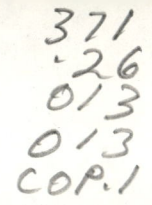

THE WINDSOR EARLY IDENTIFICATION PROJECT REVISITED

Junior Kindergarten Findings and Follow-up
of Original Kindergarten Sample

K. G. O'BRYAN, Principal Investigator

This research report was funded under contract by the Ministry of Education, Ontario.
It reflects the views of the authors and not necessarily those of the Ministry

Hon. Bette Stephenson, M.D., Minister
Dr. H. K. Fisher, Deputy Minister

© The Minister of Education, Ontario, 1980
Queen's Park
Toronto, Ontario

MINISTRY OF EDUCATION, ONTARIO CATALOGUING IN PUBLICATION

O'Bryan, K. G.
   The Windsor Early Identification Project revisited : Junior Kindergarten findings and follow-up of original Kindergarten sample / K. G. O'Bryan

   "This research project was funded under contract by the Ministry of Education, Ontario."
   Bibliography: p.

1. Windsor Early Identification Project. 2. Educational tests and measurements - Ontario - Research. 3. Prediction of scholastic success. I. Ontario. Ministry of Education. II. Title.

ON001655   371.26013   UTLAS: 54010359

ISBN 0-7743-4936-0

Additional copies may be ordered from:

Publications Sales
The Ontario Institute for Studies in Education
252 Bloor Street West
Toronto, Ontario
M5S 1V6

or from:

The Ontario Government Bookstore
880 Bay Street
Toronto, Ontario
M7A 1L2

1 2 3 4 5   48 38 28 18 08

Contents

	Abstract	i
I	Early Identification of Learning Difficulties	1
II	Review of Literature	3
	(A) Very Early Identification	7
	(B) Early Identification of Psychopathologies and Psychoneurological Disabilities	9
	(C) Early Identification of Medical and Neurological Problems	13
	(C) Early Identification of Learning Difficulty	15
III	A Brief Review of the Windsor Early Identification Project	21
IV	The Current Research	25
	(A) Assessment of the Usefulness of the W.E.I.P. in Junior Kindergarten	25
	(B) Results of the Assessment of the Usefulness of the W.E.I.P. in the Junior Kindergarten Class	26
	(C) The Current Status of the W.E.I.P. in Windsor	31
	(D) Results of Analysis of the Current Status of the W.E.I.P. in Windsor	33
	Appendix I - Modified Version of W.E.I.P.	42
	Appendix II - Report of the Consultant to the W.E.I.P., Part II	51
	Annotated Bibliography	55
	Bibliography	78

Abstract

The Windsor Early Identification Project had achieved considerable success as a viable early means of inexpensively identifying high risk/high potential children in the kindergarten year. It had been carefully researched in the initial phases (W.E.I.P., 1975) but no follow-up study had been formally attempted. Relatively little was known about its usefulness at the beginning or end of the Junior Kindergarten year. Furthermore, the subsequent progress of the children identified in the project's experimental year had not been analysed. Consequently a rich and potentially useful body of highly relevant data which had been carefully recorded for the past three years had not been assessed.

Although the establishment of an identification procedure for the Kindergarten child may provide a fairly direct adaptation potential for the Junior Kindergarten school beginner, Piaget's work suggested that marked transitions can occur in children's cognitive processes around the beginning of school and many curriculum specialists have suggested the need for care in the testing of and programming for children in the transitional stages. Therefore, it was considered necessary to assess and test adaptations in the procedure when the W.E.I.P. is used at the earlier levels. It was felt that both the items and scoring procedures might need some adjustment.

Accordingly, a study of the Windsor Early Identification Project's longitudinal results was conducted. The study was designed to provide:

(i) An updating of results obtained from Kindergarten through Grade 3 of the original final full sample of the 504 W.E.I.P. experimental children in 16 schools.

(ii) An assessment of the referral data, special education, and educational assessment outcomes of children identified by the W.E.I.P.

(iii) A renaming and revalidation of the W.E.I.P. for downward extension to the Junior Kindergarten, or for application to children who have experienced Junior Kindergarten.

Procedures used included multiple linear regression analysis of currently scored data, case study procedures, interview and observational analysis inventories, reliability and validity assessments, and decision theory analysis such as were employed in the development of the W.E.I.P.

Results showed that the Windsor Project was performing very effectively for Kindergarten identification as designed, and that the stability of the program was high. Interview data indicated that treatment approaches to identified children remained in the hands of the classroom teacher assisted by consultants from the School Board, but that no direct or systematic programming based upon identification profiles existed.

Attempts to test and redesign the W.E.I.P. for use in the Junior Kindergarten provided data which were interpreted as evidence that the current assessment battery of the W.E.I.P. was unsuitable for use in Junior Kindergarten, although the parent/teacher interview data could be taken at that time. It

was recommended that the Assessment Battery be used at the
beginning of Kindergarten rather than at the beginning or
end of Junior Kindergarten. It was further reported that
the W.E.I.P. appears to have sound longitudinal characteristics
with good predictive validity.

Early Identification of Learning Difficulties

Introduction

Early identification of children with potential learning problems has occupied a central role in special and general education over the last two decades. Most attempts have centred on the development of tests or test batteries aimed at predicting subsequent difficulties in school subjects, primarily in reading and mathematics.

Literature from both educational and psychological studies indicates that a broad range of factors are involved in the development of a learning difficulty in a child. Any one of these factors in isolation or any small clustering of them is unlikely to account for or be predictive of a subsequent general failure in school or a specific difficulty in reading or mathematics. Consequently, educators can no longer be satisfied with the use of a specific single-factor test designed to identify the child who will experience difficulty learning, whether it be to read, spell, socialize, or handle early mathematics.

Early identification is considered by many educators to be particularly desirable when it is directed towards a general assessment of the child's current capabilities, performance, behaviour patterns, prior experience, and ability to participate in the immediately planned program. The main purpose of early identification may well be the discovery of the child's current difficulties, strengths, deficits, and needs in order to provide a program beginning at the level of his available competence. The prediction of future levels of attainment should not be more than a secondary aspect of an early identification study.

The identification approach may be professionally conducted by school or independent psychologists using formal, standardized tests in a clinical setting, or may be teacher/child centred so that the professional in the applied setting becomes the key to the identification program; or it may combine both professional and applied professional approaches. Whichever basic approach is attempted, all should be supported by both medical and social data to provide the necessary context for assessment of the child's current preparedness for subsequent learning experiences. Identification programs may best serve their purpose by concentrating on providing immediate, direct, and easy-to-use information drawn from a wide variety of sources (past and present), to focus on the child's current abilities and needs. The teacher, given this type of information, is then in a position to adopt and adapt programs and strategies which may well prevent subsequent learning difficulties.

The literature is very broad in the area of learning difficulties but much less extensive on the question of early identification. The review which follows considers the key areas, and on pages 55-77 there is an extensive annotated bibliography drawn from several computer and other reference sources and reported directly.

II Review of Literature

The question of early identification has gained increasing prominence in recent years. The entries on bibliographic services have doubled in number since 1975 and have considerably broadened in scope, thus further tending to confuse an already complex issue.

Essentially, early identification might be broken down into at least the following categories:

(a) Very early identification dealing with infants and children below 4 years old.

(b) Early identification of psychopathological problems and psychoneurological disabilities.

(c) Early identification of medical and neurological problems.

(d) Early identification of educational difficulty.

The literature, of course, crosses these divisions but tends to focus study by study, primarily in one or the other of them. Consequently the review which follows is organized on the basis of the categories noted above. Most of this literature is post-1975 with the addition of a few key studies prior to that date.

Much of the earlier literature was cross-disciplinary in nature and scope, and a great proportion of it centred on the area of reading disability, particularly that which dealt with suspected minimal brain damage or with various forms of clinical dyslexia.

Dyslexia was first recognized in adults who had demonstrable brain damage due to trauma or infection and whose ability to read was totally lost or vastly impaired. The recognition of similar symptoms in children attempting to acquire reading skills opened the field to neurological and other investigations. There has since been a plethora of research in this field, but the prevalence of the problem was perhaps best illustrated by Worden and Snyder (1969) when they reported that childhood dyslexia or "specific learning disability" was currently receiving sufficient professional attention to be considered a common problem.

Incidence estimates of dyslexia ranged between two and twenty percent of the elementary school population according to Cleary (1968), but neurological findings in children were found to be not conclusive when there was average or better intelligence, where senses were unimpaired, and when motivation was high. The inconclusiveness and apparent contradictory nature of these results led many investigators, including Frostig, Kephart, Cruickshank, and Getman (Chaney and Kephart, 1968), to postulate various related theories. These were often based upon psychological, optometric, or partly physical-education concepts. The positions taken did not always arise from observed data, and there was considerable controversy generated on the validity of the diagnostic procedures (Deno, 1966).

There had been an immense amount of work done by many researchers in the field of disabilities, and Clements (1966) compiled a list of approximately one hundred specific behaviours described as learning disorders. This was done on the basis of a review of a similar number of publications, and it led Clements to cite 10 most frequent characteristics of learning disorders. These were:

- Hyperactivity
- Perceptual-motor impairments
- Emotional lability
- General orientation defects
- Disorders of attention (e.g. short attention span, distractibility)
- Impulsivity
- Disorders of memory and thinking
- Specific learning disabilities in reading, arithmetic, writing and spelling
- Disorders of speech and hearing
- Equivocal neurological signs and electro-encephalographic irregularities

McCarthy and McCarthy (1971) suggested three common elements in this list, which they presented as follows:

(1) All referred to children who were retarded or disordered in school subjects, speech, or language and/or who display behaviour problems.

(2) None were assignable to major categories of exceptionality such as mental retardation or deafness.

(3) All had some presumed neurological basis (cerebral dysfunction) for their manifest disabilities.

As a result of these studies, Clements produced a set of guidelines for examining children in order to identify as early as possible those who might eventually suffer difficulties in learning in school. These were based partly on personal data including medical, development, and family/

social histories; physical examinations; special examinations, tests, and investigations for specific medical problems. A second part of Clements's basic approach was given over to a behavioural assessment which included the recording of the academic history of the child, a psychological assessment, and language and educational testing.

There was a notable absence in the literature of specific information on the sex, age-group, and place in the school of those labelled as having a specific learning disability. In addition, there was scanty - if any - information on such children concerning the status of hearing, vision, or other physical conditions then present, the history of premature birth or allergies, and the social history of the family - all of which might be considered likely to affect early school performance.

Furthermore, the effect and incidence of such factors as perceptual motor handicap on early reading problems was beginning to be questioned. In the literature of the later 1970's it becomes apparent that early school failure in general and reading failure in particular might indeed be a result of a multiplicity of factors including the system of education itself as well as the prior experience, language skills, behavioural characteristics, and health status of the learner. Consequently, much recent literature focusses upon multiple-factor causation of potential learning problems. The Windsor study is one such multiple-factor approach taken in an applied setting.

(A)   Very Early Identification

Typical of very early identification procedures is that of Boothman et al. (1976). A test based upon developmental approaches was administered to children aged 4 weeks and repeated at 16, 28, and 52 weeks. A follow-up was completed at 3 years. Some support for the test's ability to find, very early, the children who would be slow developers was indicated. Generally, this study suggested that some benefit might be gained through early educational and health support intervention.

Very early identification of a different sort was examined by Taylor (1976) in dealing with deaf children. The five-year longitudinal study examined the usefulness of such measures as EEG, GSR, and behavioural tests for deafness and provided suggestions for early parent intervention in cases identified as hearing difficulty.

Touwen et al. (1977) evaluated the reliability of a quick screening procedure to select infants for a more detailed neurological assessment for suspected abnormalities. They reported that of the 48 infants who as a result of the screening were then given the comprehensive examination, 25 showed definite deviant neurological signs; the other 23 proved normal. Four of the 52 infants screened as normal showed slight neurological deviations during the comprehensive assessment. The authors believed that these results underlined the fact that neurological screening, while useful in selecting those infants who need further investigation, could not replace a comprehensive examination.

The work of such early childhood investigators as White (1973) suggests the very pervasive influence of home factors and particularly the influence of the mother in the subsequent performance of the child in educational settings and psychological development. The quality of the mother's interaction with the child in the years prior to 3 was considered critical.

Loss (1976), in a study involving 389 preschool children, found the following five variables to significantly discriminate high risk children: word knowledge, verbal memory-rote, sound blending, auditory reception, and quantitative (understanding of quantity concepts).

Hollinshead (1975) evaluated a program designed to make an early diagnosis of the emotional problems and learning disabilities of 40 preschool children, and to furnish educational interventions so that these problems might be ameliorated before the children entered formal schooling. The program centred around speech and language, perceptual motor activities, and adjustment to peers and adults. Evaluation objectives focussed on assessment of improvement of 50% of the participants in areas of language, perceptual motor development, social and emotional behaviour, and attitudes toward and relationships with adults in the educational setting. Pre- and post-test data revealed that statistically significant differences in the direction of gains and improvement were obtained. There was also close agreement between staff members that over 75% of the children had improved moderately or markedly in attitudes toward and relationships with adults.

These and a number of earlier studies suggest that very early identification of potential learning difficulty is possible and that a multivariate approach is the most likely to provide strong predictive correlates.

(B)   Early Identification of Psychopathologies and Psychoneurological Disabilities

In 1975 Bechtel reported the final two years of a program which provided identification and remediation services for 60 potentially dyslexic preschool children and 45 dyslexic elementary grade children. Described for the preschool program were materials and evaluative devices and methods of remediation which stressed development of perceptual motor skills, applied skills, gross motor skills, and free play. Findings were detailed showing that the experimental group made 44 positive gains (out of 50 possible test scores) over the control group, 27 of which were significant (especially in such areas as the Wechsler Full Scale IQ, letter discrimination, word discrimination, copying, and figure ground perception). It was explained that methods of remediation in the six-week program for elementary grade dyslexic students included daily instruction in reading, perceptual motor skills, gross motor skills, English composition, and mathematics, as well as weekly field trips. Conclusions showing that experimental students gained significantly over control students in such areas as figure ground perception, arithmetic computation, reading accuracy, and visual tracking were noted.

Bechtel's study was one of the few well-designed attempts to provide remediation based upon identification, and the apparent success obtained suggests a possible procedure for intervention.

A wide-ranging study of potential learning problems was presented by Jacobs and Sacatsh (1975). They examined potential learning problems and learning styles in 131 Kindergarten children through the assessment of global intelligence, gross and fine motor skills, visual perception skills, auditory perception skills, speech and language development, social skills, alphabet recognition, and number concepts. Standardized tests and informal assessment measures were used. They reported that the program distinguished five groups of children ranging from children needing gross motor or language experiences to children ready for the pre-reading program.

Becker (1976) studied the importance of regulation of conceptual tempo as a dimension of educational risk for identification of children with learning problems in 60 Kindergarten children. Risk and nonrisk children (selected on the basis of behavioural observation and teacher ratings) were compared for impulsivity and ability to regulate tempo in situations of varying levels of task complexity and under varying sets of instructions. Results suggested that risk children were more impulsive than nonrisk children, and were also less able to alter tempo when going from simple to complex situations and when told to work fast or to work slowly.

Margolis (1976) examined, with 93 Kindergarten subjects, the use of the Kindergarten Auditory Screening Test (KAST) as an effective predictor of reading disability. Results from a comparison of correlation coefficients for the KAST with the Metropolitan Readiness Test given in Kindergarten and the Gates MacGinitie Reading Tests (Primary Form) given in first grade indicated that the KAST was an inadequate screening device for the sample studied. Of course, this presupposes that the Gates MacGinitie test is an accurate criterion test. Margolis's finding is interesting, however, in that it provides evidence that the KAST does not predict well to a nationally established test.

Spalding (1972), in a key study designed to validate the effectiveness of the Quick Neurological Screening Test (QNST), compared the performance of 88 elementary and high school children identified as learning disabled with 88 matched controls. It was concluded that the QNST measured neurological signs which differentiate between learning disabled and normal children.

Another quick screening device did not fare so well when tested by Rogers and Richmond (1975). Although this was conducted on older children and adults, the results are an interesting example of the difficulties encountered in this work. Fifty-four subjects were administered the Slosson Drawing Coordination Test (SDCT) and the Bender Visual Motor Gestalt test. Twenty-nine subjects were labelled possibly brain damaged by the SDCT, and 17 subjects by the M. Hutt scoring system for the Bender-Gestalt. Two psychologists using all available data and clinical judgment classified only 13 in a similar category. Results indicated the need for caution in using the SDCT as a screening instrument for brain damage.

Similar cautions in the use of such tests were advised by Silverman and O'Bryan (1973) in their report of a perceptual motor handicap study. Nevertheless, substantial controversy still exists in the use of psychometric tests for identifying minimal brain dysfunction.

Again using older children, Brenton and Gilmore (1976) developed and tested, with 50 male and 10 female elementary school students (6 to 13 years old) who were legally identified as learning disabled, an index of discrepancy to assist in determining an operational definition of learning disabilities in the cognitive domain. The index, derived from the Full Scale IQ score of the Wechsler Intelligence Scale for Children and relevant subtest scores on the Peabody Individual Achievement Test, identified 74% of the male subjects and 30% of the female subjects as possibly learning disabled in the cognitive domain.

Such findings are common in the literature, but very often fail to replicate when attempted by other researchers or when similar approaches are used. For example, Neel (1976) studied a group of 120 children with academic difficulties to determine specific subpopulations by use of psychometric measures. The subjects, clinically identified as having academic difficulties, came from the Switzer Center for Educational Therapy and were selected by age (6-9) and IQ scores. Staff psychologists administered the Wechsler Intelligence Scale for Children, Illinois Test of Psycholinguistic Abilities, Frostig Developmental Test of Visual Perception, and Wepman Auditory Discrimination to subjects who were then classified into groups according to selected variables. Their scores were factor analysed to determine whether or not specific identifying variables could be determined. Four factors were found: intelligence, visual, language, and auditory. Performance and verbal scores on the WISC did not seem to differentiate specific subpopulations of children with academic difficulties, although the WISC remains a very useful test of performance variables in the verbal and non-verbal domain.

It would seem from the bulk of the literature (more of which is summarized in the Annotated Bibliography presented later in this report) that the definitions of psychopathological and psychoneurological disabilities are still very much an open question.

(C)   Early Identification of Medical and Neurological Problems

There appears to be greater security of research in early identification of problems of the medical and neurological type. This type of research has substantial implications for the present review in that the Windsor Study has major medical components.

Sterling and Sterling in two studies (1977a and b) examined the use of the Quick Neurological Screening Test, the Denver Developmental Screening Test, and complete physical examinations for over 250 preschool and primary students. It was found that the DDST identified only 17% of children found by physical examination to have organic neurological disorders, while 56% of children with neurological disorders successfully passed all four DDST subtests.

In the second study, in order to investigate associations between vestibular function, balance, and related neurodevelopmental or neurophysiological test results and learning success or failure, each of 66 children with learning disorders was given an assessment which included the QNST. Findings suggested an empirical relationship between QNST subtest results (particularly those relating to balance) and auditory receptive skills.

Levin and Erber (1976) conducted a school-wide vision screening program to identify correctable and uncorrectable visual abnormalities in 165 children (4-16 years old). Another purpose of the screening program was to evaluate a variety of simple vision tests that could be administered by nonmedical personnel, in order to assemble a test battery appropriate for screening children with limited language. Tests of distant and near visual acuity, binocular vision (depth perception and fusion), color vision, and peripheral vision were evaluated. Most of the tests were found to be useful in identifying visual deficiencies in hearing impaired children 4 years of age and older.

Also in the field of hearing impairment Fisher (1976) investigated the efficiency and effectiveness of using a portable sound-treated booth in detecting hearing impairments during screening of 350 children (Kindergarten-Grade 6) in a public school hearing conservation program. The subjects, who were first screened in an open environment and in a portable audiometric booth, were then given a threshold test in an audiometric sound-treated booth in a portable van with audiometers calibrated to standards set by the American National Standards Institute. Results indicated that there was a significant benefit in using a portable sound-treated enclosure during the initial screening to correctly identify larger percentages of students with or without hearing impairment, the major value being the reduction of wasted time spent in retesting students with normal hearing.

A massive study in Ohio conducted by Bunner on pre- and school-age children tested 3,261 preschool children and 44,885 school-age children for problems of distance visual acuity, muscle balance, and observable eye problems. Criteria were established for testing procedures and referrals. Forty-two percent of the estimated preschool population was tested, and 205 children referred for further testing. Follow-up investigations revealed that over 90% of the referred children had received eye examinations and treatment. Only first-grade children were tested for hyperopia, and 33 of the 95 children referred would not have received treatment had they only been tested for visual acuity.

Studies such as these reflect the power of research directed towards early identification factors beyond the direct scope of education; however, the prime concern of this report deals with attempts to identify the child who might have problems in the classroom. Accordingly, this final section of the review of literature examines the early identification of learning problems in the pre- and early school years.

(D)   Early Identification of Learning Difficulty

The Windsor Early Identification Project (O'Bryan, 1976) was based upon a multivariate approach using applied professionals as testers. Several recent studies have tended to go this route, but the literature reports mainly those studies conducted by psycho-educational researchers. One such was by Colligan (1977), who sought to determine the value of the Pupil Rating Scale in identifying children at risk for learning difficulty. A sample of 60 Kindergarten children was studied intensively to determine whether the Pupil Rating Scale would correlate as well with achievement measures as reported in Myklebust's normative sample. The study included one group test designed to measure general learning readiness (Metropolitan Readiness Test), a group test more clearly tied to specific mastery of prereading tasks (Lippincott Reading Readiness Test), and individual assessment of each child's knowledge of letters and numbers. The significant correlations with these measures of outcome provided considerable support for the use of the Pupil Rating Scale in a Kindergarten population, according to Colligan.

Another study using the Myklebust scale as a marker was conducted by Federici et al. (1976), who tested with 580 first-grade urban Black subjects the Meeting Street School Screening Test (MSSST) and the Myklebust Pupil Rating Scale for the early identification of children with potential learning problems. Results supported the use of the tests with this population in that (1) the MSSST identified the same proportion (15%) of high risk subjects in the experimental group that is estimated for the general population, (2) the Myklebust discriminated between high risk (N=22) and low risk (N=21) subjects within the minority group using the MSSST as the criterion variable, and (3) Myklebust ratings for the subjects approximated ratings reported elsewhere for older White suburban subjects.

Handicapped children were studied by Magliocca et al. (1977) in a pilot study initiated with three regular preschool classes (65 children) to determine the validity of identifying preschool handicapped children (3½ to 5½ years of age) through a frequency sampling technique. The frequencies of correct responses of each child on the nine one-minute academic tasks (e.g. matching colours) were counted. A list of at-risk learners was developed consisting of all children performing in the lower 25% of frequency scores. Three conclusions emerged from the study: (1) the amount of instructional time saved through screening is critical; (2) teacher variables were not an issue in the screening; and (3) the predictive validity of screening through a frequency sampling technique is high.

A major early identification approach was one used by Merenda et al. (1977). They conducted a project involving 851 children in grades Kindergarten through 2 to determine the reliability of the Rhode Island Pupil Identification Scale (RIPIS), a behaviour observation scale for identifying young children with learning problems. Detailed are analyses of data regarding internal consistency, stability of individual subscale scores, stability of Part I and Part II profiles, and homogeneity of Part I and Part II total scores. Results were said to indicate that all subscales, profiles, and composites were highly internally consistent and stable over a five-month period.

Of importance to the Windsor Project was a study conducted by Zahn (1975), who found in a study involving 224 Kindergarten children that brief screening tests can be valid detectors of Kindergarten children with perceptual and learning problems, and that the incidence of hyperkinesis in Kindergarten children diminishes as the occurrence of perceptual difficulty decreases.

Similar results were discovered by Bach (1975) with older children to whom Metropolitan Achievement tests had been administered together with a battery of five tests of cognitive processes. The relationship between scores in the verbal and nonverbal portions of the battery was seen to have utility in providing economical screening and preliminary diagnosis of patterns of underachievement.

Social factors are also considered to be directly related to the problem of early identification; thus a study by Van Doorninck et al. (1976) had marked implications for the W.E.I.P. These authors conducted a follow-up study of 151 lower socioeconomic class children (under 6 years of age at the time of initial screening) to determine the effectiveness of the Denver Developmental Screening Test (DDST) in predicting school achievement problems. Subjects were originally categorized into three age groups (0 to 2 years, 2 to 4 years, and 4 to 6 years) and three DDST classifications (normal, questionable, and abnormal). Follow-up evaluation (which took place when subjects' school placement ranged from beginning Kindergarten to Grade 5) included the following: achievement test percentiles, grade placement or special education status, and teacher ratings on the school Behaviour Check List. Based on the above data, subjects were classified as having school problems if they met one or more of four criteria (which included achievement test percentiles of 10 or less).

Results indicated that the majority of subjects categorized as nonnormal had later school problems and that prediction became more accurate with increasing age of screening in abnormals.

Another follow-up study on a different variable was done by Forness et al. (1976). From a prior Kindergarten population sample, 61 first-grade students were involved in a follow-up study to determine the validity of observable classroom behaviour evaluations in predicting educational risk. Teacher ratings and individual achievement test scores at follow-up for the children originally classified into four behavioural clusters (ranking risk) showed that the nonrisk cluster continued to do well, while high risk children were doing poorly in some areas; and that children in a cluster originally viewed as nonrisk were also having difficulty in school.

Bell et al. (1977) in a major research investigated reading retardation. A 12-year longitudinal study involving almost 1,000 Kindergarten children, including normal and learning disabled students, was conducted to assess the predictive efficiency of a preschool test battery in relation to short- and long-term school achievement, to evaluate socioeconomic locale and operational school structure as indicators of subsequent progress, and to observe the effects of some correctional experience on later school performance. Among findings were that 23% failed to complete first-grade requirements in the first year; that failure rates within separate schools ranged from 3% to 71% and had an inverse relationship to socioeconomic level; and that within the middle-class area, children in an open-space school had double the failure rate of their peers in traditional classrooms.

Another area of major concern in early identification work is posed by the non-English-speaking student. Evans (1976) researched a series of programs designed to identify the preschool Mexican American child with existing and/or potentially handicapping conditions, to develop and test supplementary materials, and to determine the efficacy of supplementary instruction within the regular bilingual classroom. In the first project for 4-year-olds, 40 out of 99 children enrolled had some type of problem, with 29 having problems severe enough to interfere with learning. Following five months of supplementary instruction, the experimental group out-performed the comparison group not receiving supplementary instruction and were learning at the level of nonhandicapped peers. In the second project for 5-year-olds, materials for continuous observation and supplementary instruction on a lesson-by-lesson basis were developed which include two identification instruments, the Spanish/English Language Performance Screening and the Observational Checklists for Referral, and four instructional materials.

There are a great many attempts to identify older children reported in the literature, but it seems clear that the trend is to earlier and earlier identification. Hence it was decided to review the W.E.I.P. to determine whether it would be suitable for use in Junior Kindergarten. It was also felt necessary to review the longitudinal aspects of the study to follow up the original sample and so refine the current identification procedures. A report of the study follows.

III A Brief Review of the Windsor Early Identification Project

A multidisciplinary project carried out in schools of the Windsor Board of Education resulted in the development of a statistically reliable method for identifying 5-year-old Kindergarten children's problems that could affect their optimal educational attainments in school.

The research, funded by the Ontario Ministry of Education, was conducted over a four-year period, with the results published in the 1975 report of the Windsor Early Identification Project.

The project involved staff of the Windsor Board of Education and health services in the community. The research team was headed by Dr. K. G. O'Bryan, then Associate Professor of Applied Psychology at the Ontario Institute for Studies in Education.

The research led to the identification, early in the Kindergarten year, of a substantial number of children who are either low or high performers on skills that have been judged as essential to learning in school.

The involvement of educators and health personnel not only aided the research but also made possible the development of follow-up procedures. The results of these procedures were, however, not part of the original research endeavour but form the basis of the current report.

The Windsor approach consists essentially of four inter-related components - parent involvement, determination of each child's health status, identification of the educational needs of each child on entering Kindergarten, and follow-up on the problems identified.

Parent involvement was obtained by publicity, meetings, and individual contact. Appointments were made for parent and child for two occasions: initial or pre-registration in March, and the September enrolment in school. Subsequent reporting by the teacher on the child's progress follows throughout the school year.

The health status of each child was determined through the testing of hearing and vision by trained staff of the Metro Windsor-Essex County Health Unit and through a history of past and present health conditions obtained from the parent by the child's teacher. The follow-up of health problems was carried out by the Health Unit and the family physician or specialist.

In addition, an assessment of each child's speech was undertaken by speech teachers to identify any speech deficits which might become serious impediments to the child's later performance in school. The treatment of such deficits was then set in progress.

Identification of the educational needs of each child was done by the teacher at the time of enrolment in school in September. Individual appointments were made for the parent and child prior to the class meeting as a whole. This was accomplished at the rate of approximately eight appointments per day and was well received by parents. The child benefited by personal contact with the teacher and enjoyed a pleasant introduction to the school environment.

The status of the child's educational skills at that time in receptive language, auditory association, expressive language, number concepts, and the recognition of colours was determined by the teacher. The scores obtained by the child on each of the assessments were recorded and converted into scaled scores to determine low and high performers at that time.

As the 1975 report noted, children in Windsor schools were identified by this method so that the teacher, with assistance when necessary from Primary Division consultants and Special Education staff, could undertake the development of individual programs for both the low-performing and gifted children.

The children were followed throughout the Kindergarten year, and a test for readiness to read was administered by the teacher at the end of that year to assist in the placement of the child the following year. The continuing progress of each participant in the project was monitored through Grades 1, 2, and 3; therefore, the continuing children from the original full sample provided the data for the report which follows.

An important aspect of the project is the simplified method of recording all information obtained for the use of the teacher and the development of a continuous record of a child's progress. The latter has been put into operation by the Computer Services of the Windsor Board, with parental consent, for the retention of educational information. These records are available to parents on request; otherwise, strict confidentiality is maintained.

The Report on the Early Identification Program of the Board of Education of Windsor, 1974-78 (Vivian, 1979)) combines a visual presentation by scaled scores in charts from the Kindergarten assessment to placement in September 1978.

IV The Current Research

(A) Assessment of the Usefulness of the W.E.I.P. in Junior Kindergarten

The research was conducted in two phases. Phase I dealt with an attempt to revise the Windsor Early Identification Project for use in Junior Kindergarten classes. To this end a research design was proposed to assess the current battery in modified form. It was planned to test 100 Junior Kindergarten children with a specially revised technique. The sample was expected to be composed of 50 boys and 50 girls in two equal groups of 50 each. The first group was to receive a pre-test of the W.E.I.P. which would then be further revised for post-testing on a follow-up group. As the results reported later will indicate, it soon became apparent that the W.E.I.P., as it currently is constructed, cannot effectively be used in the Junior Kindergarten.

Initially, a sample of 64 Junior Kindergarten children participated in the testing, which was conducted by a single trained tester using a W.E.I.P. kit and a standard procedure. Testing proceeded over a one-month period in the spring term of 1979. Each child was tested individually, and appropriate modifications in the acceptability of the answers were permitted. Reliability checks were made by using split-half and test-retest approaches after a two-day delay. As will be noted, these proved to be indicative of research difficulty. Subsequently, a modified W.E.I.P., containing the changes noted in Appendix I, was created and tested on 50 additional children. Results obtained indicated several problems with the approach taken.

(B)   Results of the Assessment of the Usefulness of the W.E.I.P. in the Junior Kindergarten Class

Almost from the beginning of the data collection, it became apparent that the assessment battery of the W.E.I.P. was not an effective tool, in its present form, for use in the Junior Kindergarten in academic assessment. There was no problem, however, in using the materials other than the assessment battery. The parent report forms are quite effective, and all other non-child-produced data are most adequate. The basic problem encountered was the children's inability to appropriately respond to the test materials. It proved very difficult indeed to obtain any consistency in the answers of the children, even though actual scaled scores approached an expected mean (Table 1). Very few children scored high on the scales, and a disproportional number (by Kindergarten standards) were at the "at risk" level.

The tester reported that the children tended to answer randomly, and that reasons for answers were clearly lacking. This view was confirmed by the principal investigator's testing of additional children, many of whom were clearly insufficiently mature to adequately respond to the materials as presented.

Table 1

Mean Scores Obtained for Unmodified (UM) and Modified (M) W.E.I.P. Assessment on First Testing

	Colour		Rec. Lang.		Exp. Lang.		Aud. Ass.		Math	
	M	UM	M	UM	M	UM	M	UM	M	UM
x̄	3.2	2.5	3.4	2.9	3.3	2.5	2.9	2.5	3.0	2.7
n	50	64	50	64	50	64	50	64	50	64

Reliability figures showed a very disappointing split-half coefficient of .34, which clearly reflected the view of the tester that the majority of the children were not taking the test as designed but were scoring on chance or other variability factors. Test-retest figures were equally low as all reliability coefficients failed to reach .4. This is in sharp contrast to the W.E.I.P. in which reliability was consistently high.

The low reliability made any validity factors untenable since reliability of a sufficient level (at least .6) is required for meaningful assessment.

Consequently it must be concluded that the W.E.I.P. as it is currently structured is not suitable for use in the early months of Junior Kindergarten.

When a modified version, reducing the number and range and simplifying the language of the original questions, was developed (Appendix I), it too failed to produce responses that could be relied upon to provide a fair assessment of the children tested. The youngsters were clearly not being tested on items appropriate to their level of experience; and consequently, reliability coefficients again failed to reach .4 on either split-half or test-retest calculations. Again, such low reliability invalidated any attempts to match the teacher ratings to the obtained scores.

Several reasons can be suggested for the failure of either the current or the modified version of the W.E.I.P. Assessment Battery in Junior Kindergarten.

The W.E.I.P. was formulated expressly for older children, taking into account their developmental and experiential level and matching those variables to the expected activity and educational demands of the Kindergarten year. It was designed by Kindergarten specialists for use with Kindergarten entrants. The language used was suitable to 5-year-olds, not 4-year-olds, and the concepts involved presupposed knowledge of and exposure to activities and ideas up to and including the fifth year of life, so that a normally developing and educationally able child of 5 could score at least at the mean.

It achieved its high reliability because, basically, the questions asked were appropriate to its target audience. It failed to achieve reliability with the 4-year-olds for perhaps the same reason, but this time in the negative sense in that the questions were inappropriate to the developmental and experiential level of the 4-year-old child.

A second reason has to do with the nature of the performance being predicted to. The W.E.I.P. had, as its criterion, performance in the Kindergarten year, a year which is structurally quite different from Junior Kindergarten. Junior Kindergarten places much less academic demand on its children. Most of the experience is psychosocial and psychomotor, and it is clear that such a program demands pre-testing of these experiences if any attempt to predict performance is to have even minimal chance of success. Furthermore, structural changes or modifications were ineffective because the basic questions asked in the W.E.I.P. were not appropriate to the Junior Kindergarten experience. Therefore, a substantially re-designed set of questions based upon the five assessment areas together with other facets would be required to fairly test for learning difficulty identification in Junior Kindergarten.

Such a newly defined assessment battery could follow the format of the W.E.I.P. A selected group of Junior Kindergarten teachers would first create potential test items for inclusion in a preliminary assessment battery. The preliminary battery would then be subjected to reliability and validity testing as was done in the Windsor Project (O'Bryan, 1975). Such an approach would offer some possibility of obtaining a successful test battery.

However, it is questionable whether the use of an early identification package for educational assessment of the 4-year-old school beginner is a wise undertaking. This question arises out of a third factor noted in the course of testing for this study. It seems clear that the younger child needs a much more clinical type of assessment procedure - the standardized approach does not work well enough to justify quantitative result interpretation. Many children perceive what appears to be a straightforward question in a much different way from that perceived by the questioner. For example, one respondent on being asked the question "If Mummy puts down 4 cookies, and Billy takes one of them, how many are left?" replied, "There'd be three, but I don't know who Billy is!" Although the correct answer was given mathematically, it was apparent that the respondent viewed the problem as something other than pure math. It is clearly important that the teacher or tester be aware of these differences.

It is felt that extreme caution should be exercised in assessing the educational potential (as opposed to the current educational status) of the Junior Kindergarten child. Accordingly, an alternative approach is proposed.

In the judgment of the author, the following procedure is justified on the data obtained on the W.E.I.P. and from the current study:

> The non-educational assessments (the social history; hearing, vision, and speech screening; health history; and any parent interviews and teacher observations) may be conducted in the Junior Kindergarten year. This can be at the option of the educational authority concerned and is unlikely to be misleading, since all reporting or assessing is done by the teacher or by the parent to the teacher. However, the Assessment Battery of the W.E.I.P. should not be administered in its current form in Junior Kindergarten.

Substantial benefit can be derived from the use of those parts of the W.E.I.P. not including the assessment battery. Many reports from Windsor Board of Education teachers and other users stress the value of the parent-teacher interview for the contacts it provides for all concerned as well as for its useful socio-medical content. There seems no reason why such a useful procedure should not be adopted in both Senior Kindergarten and Junior Kindergarten years, especially if the interview in Kindergarten is used to update or revise the information obtained earlier.

Overall, it is the author's conclusion that the assessment battery is highly effective in use in the Kindergarten, and that the best place for the full package is at the beginning of the Kindergarten year.

(C) The Current Status of the W.E.I.P. in Windsor

The basic requirements for this section of the study were as follows:

 (a) To examine the longer-term validity and reliability of the W.E.I.P. procedures, including the performance testing, the medical and social histories, and the teacher evaluations.

 (b) To assess the relationships between the major extremes of identification (High Risk/High Performance) of children in the final year of the project (1974-75) and their performance in Grades 1, 2, and 3. The purpose of this procedure was to examine and refine the longer-term prediction and identification capacity of the procedure.

(c) To analyse the performance of the children who were identified as potentially high risk and whose subsequent school record resulted in referrals to psychological or special-class treatment. This required a case study approach and was intended to serve as a basis for development of correlated treatment packages for use with the early identification procedures.

(d) To examine the feasibility and adaptations necessary to assess the W.E.I.P. procedures for use in Junior Kindergarten or in subsequent modified applications.

Methods

The study employed two basic research methodologies:
(a) a revisit to the computerized records of the children involved in the project, and
(b) a case study analysis of all referrals to any form of special or extra treatment.

Computer Analysis

All continuing records of the children included in the final year of the W.E.I.P. are held in the computer storage of the Windsor Board of Education. Continuous testing in reading, math, language, and behavioural variables

has been conducted according to the approaches laid down
in the original study. These proved to be a very rich data
source requiring only a program/writing and data analysis
to provide an excellent source of validation of the W.E.I.P.
The following procedures were employed:

    (i)   Prediction correlation beginning in Kindergarten 1974 to the end of 1978 in terms of High Risk/ High Performance children on all W.E.I.P. variables as the contributing variables, with dependent variables being performance scores at the completion of reading readiness through Grade 3. These dependent variables included reading, language, math; psychological adjustment; attention; other factors including allergies, speech, vision, and hearing.

    (ii)   Case studies of all referrals to special services. Historical analysis of all data but primarily performance and behavioural information obtained during Kindergarten W.E.I.P. testing and followed during reading readiness through Grade 3.

    (iii)   Collection of information on teacher-based in-classroom intervention programs for identified children.

(D)   Results of Analysis of the Current Status of the W.E.I.P. in Windsor

There seems little question that the W.E.I.P. has performed remarkably well in the task of assessing children at risk in the first year of formal education. It has been equally successful in indicating children likely to do very well in school. Table 2 presents percentages of prediction variables for children in each of the categories in terms of year-end performance.

Table 2

Performance at Year End
and Prediction Accuracy*

Year	Performance		
	High	Middle	Low
1	92%*	84%**	87%***
2	81%	79%	79%
3	73%	78%	74%
n=465			

*   Percentage correctly identified as likely to do well at school subjects.

** Percentage correctly identified as likely to do moderately well at school subjects.

*** Percentage correctly identified as likely to be at risk in school subjects.

It can be seen from the table that the assessment battery has maintained a high degree of predictability of subsequent performance based upon teacher assessments of the children's work.

Performance on the various assessment tests of reading and mathematics in each of the three years has been analysed for all 1974-75 children currently remaining in the Windsor system. Four hundred and sixty-five cases were available for study, and the data indicate that the prediction of performance was very accurate to the end of Grade 1, exceeding 84% in all categories. But this falls somewhat to the order of 80% in Grade 2, and to approximately 75% accuracy at Grade 3. In all cases the chi square is greater than .001. So there can be little or no doubt that the W.E.I.P. is a very powerful early identification package.

Where prediction fails it appears to fail principally among those children who gained very low initial scores as a result of being of a mother tongue other than English. Many such children performed relatively poorly in Kindergarten and Grade 1 until their knowledge of English consolidated sufficiently to enable them to take advantage of the school's offerings.

This is a most important factor for at least two reasons. In the first instance it explains the drop in prediction in the latter years, and secondly it indicates the need for caution by the assessing teacher in interpreting data obtained from children whose first language is not English. Such children may be given the tests, but care should be taken to interpret the results in the light of possible temporary deficits in language comprehension.

The data obtained from children still in the Windsor system suggest that the multiple linear regression prediction of the full assessment battery to each of the criteria ranges between .45 and .69 over the three years. All of these correlations are highly significant statistically and suggest that the W.E.I.P. is a stable and valid predictor of learning difficulty in the elementary school years. However, the referral to special education of children at high risk and the effect of deficit-recovery from English as a second language have served to reduce these correlations somewhat artificially; consequently they should be regarded as least estimates of the power of the test to accurately predict performance.

Table 3 presents data available from 21 children who scored less than 10 of a possible 25 on the Kindergarten assessment and whose scores were available for Grade 1 and Grade 2 assessment in math, reading comprehension, and word analysis.

Table 3

Comparison of Scores Obtained by Children
Identified as Very High Risk in 1974-75
with Scores Obtained by the Same Children
in Subsequent Testing

$\bar{x}$ Kindergarten Assessment					$\bar{x}$ Grade 1			$\bar{x}$ Grade 2			n=21
Col.	RL	AA	EL	M	M	RC	WA	M	RC	WA	
1.3	1.4	1.4	0.9	1.2	2.1	2.2	2.2	2.4	2.1	2.3	

Children who entered school with a first language other than English were excluded from this analysis. Other children who had left the system were also excluded, as were those whose performance or scores were so low that they had been referred to special education classes or other assistance and had not, therefore, taken part in longitudinal testing.

Again it is clear from the data that many children at risk appear to remain so throughout their early school career. Undoubtedly identification is but a first step which then requires adaptive programming, especially for those children not sufficiently learning disabled or impaired to require special education placement. On the other hand, the very good record of the W.E.I.P. in finding, very early, those children most in need of special education is also reflected in the referral data. If a variable called "reversal tendencies" (which was not included in the W.E.I.P. but which has been subsequently used by the Windsor Board staff as a referral variable at the end of each school year) is partially eliminated from the data, it can be seen that the W.E.I.P. accurately identified 23 of 37 referrals from Kindergarten through Grade 2. Of the remainder the W.E.I.P. appears to have identified four children as non-risk academically who were referred, but three of these were referred for reasons other than direct academic difficulty. Seven children identified as only of moderate risk and who exhibited marked reversal tendencies were given further assistance by special education consultants. In all of these cases their subsequent academic scores were remarkably accurately predicted by the W.E.I.P., with subsequent mean scores on academic tests showing consistency across subject areas and exhibiting remarkably little variability from year to year. Interestingly, the reversal tendency itself does not appear to have seriously affected the performance of the children in at least half of those referred on this variable.

The other three children are also interesting cases. One case appears to have been picked up in another category by the W.E.I.P. which identified the child as above average. However, he failed to live up to this promise in Grade 1 and moved to a new school for a year. This appeared to be a successful approach, since he has now been placed in Grade 3 and appears to be improving significantly.

Another W.E.I.P. child identified as somewhat better than average, but noted as an English as a second language child, was referred to special education with substantial success, where she has been advanced a grade as a very bright student.

The remaining child referred to special education was not identified as at risk by the W.E.I.P., and his subsequent performance seems to support the possibility that referral was unnecessary or was based upon needs other than academic performance.

What is clear from these data is that referral to special education has been made at an early age, and that the majority of those referred have been returned to the normal stream. While the data obtained could not be indicative of a general provincial trend, they do suggest that early referral and prompt attention may serve to assist children in need of additional help. Referrals overall were less than 7.5% of all entrants in the Kindergarten group, and there appears to be a substantial amount of individual programming offered by teachers involved in the project.

It is also extremely interesting to note that of 37 referrals from the original 504 cases, 9 of these were in Kindergarten; 15 in Grade 1; 5 in Grade 2; and none in Grade 3. It would certainly be going beyond the available data to suggest that the W.E.I.P. will reduce referrals and special class placement throughout all boards in which it is in use, but it does indicate a strong trend in that direction in Windsor. Furthermore, there is a good level of return to regular classrooms or continuation at adjusted progress rates.

The other end of the W.E.I.P. continuum dealt with students considered as very likely to do well in the school system. Current case study data are available for 36 of the original group of these children, all of whom scored 20 or more of a possible 25 on the educational assessment. Table 4 provides a summary of data obtained from this group through Grade 3. A quite remarkable and (for the researcher interested in "reversals" as a predictor of learning problems) a very critical phenomenon was observed. Fourteen of these very bright children exhibited marked reversal tendencies, none of which persisted into Grade 3. In fact, there is only a slightly higher rate of reversals for the at-risk children. These data suggest a strong possibility that reversals are largely a developmental phenomenon having very little value in the identification of possible learning difficulty in Kindergarten.

These data clearly show the very high stability of the W.E.I.P. assessment scores and give very good long-term grounds for believing it to be an excellent predictor of success in the early grades in school.

Table 4

Summary of Data for Children Achieving
Very High Scores in the W.E.I.P.

W.E.I.P. $\bar{x}$	Grade 1 $\bar{x}$	Grade 2 $\bar{x}$	Grade 3 $\bar{x}$
20.8	19.8	19.0	19.3

Teacher-Based Interaction

Currently, the approach taken in Windsor to the treatment of the child identified by the W.E.I.P. is very much one of reliance upon the teacher's professional judgment, supported by discussions with consultants from the Windsor Board of Education, and backed up by professional services of Special Education personnel and resources. No packaged or data-related treatment approaches have been systematically designed and evaluated. Indeed, this cannot be held to be a criticism of the W.E.I.P. itself in that the project was designed and executed exclusively as an identification procedure. But it can be considered a most necessary next step in exploiting the knowledge and experience gained in working with the W.E.I.P.

It is apparent that individual teachers and the Windsor consultants have developed a series of responses to the children identified by the W.E.I.P., but most of these are highly individualized and reflect the individual teacher's sense of what might be done. Perhaps this is an appropriate, or even the most appropriate, way to proceed; but in the absence of an evaluation procedure based upon a systematic observational study, such a conclusion cannot be reached. What does seem to be needed is a thorough and long-term study of various intervention procedures designed to produce a set of alternatives for application in the early grades, followed by an analysis of the potential generalizability of the procedures. Such an approach need not be particularly costly, since the implementation will be within the regular scope of the classroom teacher's duties, but it does need time.

The W.E.I.P. achieved its measure of success from a careful, longitudinal analysis. Subsequent treatment approaches will require similar foresight on the part of funding and participating groups.

Appendix I

Modified Version of W.E.I.P.

Since the purpose of this section of the study was to assess the possibility of a downward extension of the W.E.I.P., only slight modifications were made. Procedures remained the same as for the W.E.I.P. administered to Kindergarten children, but some items were deleted and the scoring system was made more liberal.

KNOWLEDGE OF COLOUR

Materials:

    Colour Card
    The colours on the card are arranged in the following sequence:
        <u>Side 1</u> - red, green, yellow, blue, orange, black, purple
        <u>Side 2</u> - brown, pink, white, gold, silver, violet, grey

Procedure:

    Show the child side 1.

    Say: "WHAT COLOUR IS THIS?" as each colour is pointed to from left to right.

    Continue with Side 2, pointing to each colour from left to right.

Scoring:

    Score 1 point for each colour known on the Pupil's Record Sheet. Record the total number of points. A maximum of 14 points is possible. If no colours known, record as 0.

Rating:

    Rate the child on a scale of 0 to 5 according to the number of points scored using the following guide:

No. of Points	Scaled Score
0	0
1-2	1

No. of Points	Scaled Score
3-5	2
6-8	3
9-10	4
11-14	5

RECEPTIVE LANGUAGE

Materials:

- 1 large box
- 1 small box that will fit easily into the larger box
- 2 forks
- 2 spoons
- 2 knives
- 1 primary pencil
- 4 pieces of dowelling - 3", 4", 5", 6"
- 1 piece of rope - at least ¼" in diameter and 30" long
- 2 pieces of cardboard - 7" x 8-3/4"
- 2 soft toys - teddy bear and ball

(Remove colour card, 2 pieces of cardboard, blocks, red, white and blue ball and number card from box. Set them aside.)

Procedures:

Suggested Organization of Table Materials

As far as possible the table should be set according to the plan below. The loose objects (those not in boxes) must not be arranged in groups. They would be scattered on the table in the general position indicated, but their own particular pattern may vary.

Child's Chair		Examiner's Chair

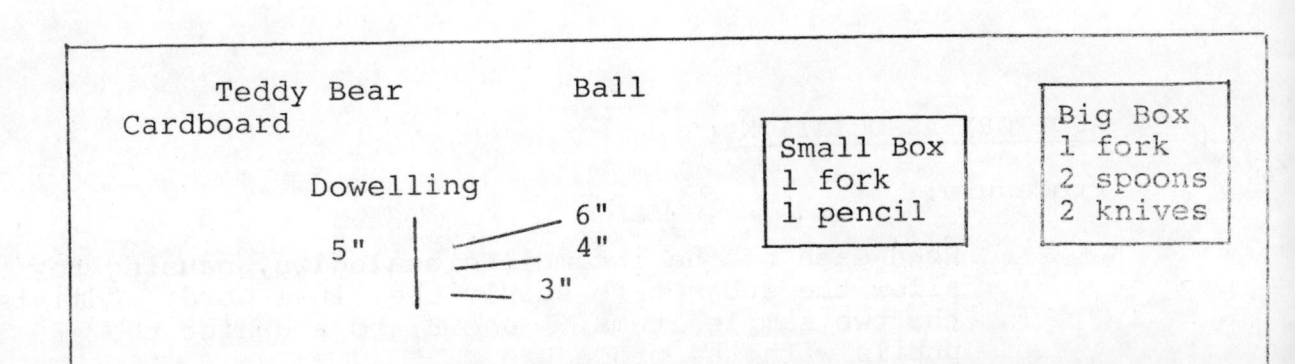

Teddy Bear Ball Cardboard Dowelling 5" 6" 4" 3"	Small Box 1 fork 1 pencil	Big Box 1 fork 2 spoons 2 knives

43

Before starting the test, say to the child, "Listen carefully, do only what I tell you to do." Start the test by asking the child to stand up. Do not score this response. Ask all the items in order. If the child fails a question or does not obey a direction, proceed to the next item. From item 2 onward correct all wrong responses. If in question 2 the child points to the small box, say, "<u>This</u> is the big box", and point to it. It is important that the child is not prevented from success on subsequent items by failure on previous ones.

Items:

1. Sit on the floor.
2. Show me the big box.
3. Take a fork out of the big box.
4. Put <u>it</u> into the small box.
5. Put <u>the</u> small box into the big box.
6. Put both boxes under the table.
7. Show me the sticks on the table.
8. Hold up the longest stick.

Scoring:

Score 1 point for each correct response on the Pupil's Record Sheet. Each item has to be completed correctly in all respects to score this point. Record total number of points. A maximum of 8 points is possible. Record as 0 if no points obtained.

Rating:

Rate the child on a scale of 0 to 5 according to the following guide:

<u>No. of Points</u>	<u>Scaled Score</u>
0	0
1-2	1
3-4	2
5-6	3
7	4
8	5

<u>AUDITORY ASSOCIATION</u>

Procedure:

Read each of the incomplete analogies, pausing to allow the subject to supply the final word. Administer the two sample items, A and B, to acquaint the pupils with the procedure.

A. Say:

"YOU SIT ON A CHAIR (point to the chair)."
"YOU SLEEP ON A _____. (bed, couch, setee, cot, bunk)."

(Pause for 5 seconds).
If the child responds incorrectly ask:

"WHERE DO YOU SLEEP?"
When the child responds, say:
"YES, YOU SLEEP ON A BED."

Repeat the analogy,

"YOU SIT ON A CHAIR."
"YOU SLEEP ON A BED."

If the child does not respond, ask:
"DO YOU SLEEP ON A BED? (couch, cot, etc.)."
When the child answers in the affirmative, repeat the analogy.

B. "WE HEAR WITH OUR EARS. (Point to ears)."
"WE SEE WITH OUR _____. (Pause for 5 seconds)."

If the child has difficulty, question as previously, and repeat the analogy.

Administer all test items.

Items:

1. I PUT A HAT ON MY HEAD: I PUT SHOES ON MY _____.

2. A RECORD IS FOR LISTENING; A BOOK IS FOR _____.

3. I SLEEP WHEN I'M TIRED; I EAT WHEN I'M _____.

4. A PILLOW IS SOFT; A STONE IS _____.

5. A WAGON HAS FOUR WHEELS; A TRICYCLE HAS _____.

6. A BIRD MAKES A NEST; A SPIDER MAKES A _____.

7. A JET IS AN AIRPLANE; A SUBMARINE IS A _____.

Scoring Guide:

1. feet
2. looking, reading
3. hungry, starved
4. hard
5. three
6. web
7. ship, boat

Scoring:

Score 1 point for each item passed on the Pupil's Record Sheet. Record points. A maximum of 7 points is possible. Score as 0 if no points are obtained.

Rating Scale:

Rate the child on a scale of 0 to 5 according to the following guide:

No. of Points	Scaled Score
0	0
1	1
2	2
3	3
4-5	4
6-7	5

EXPRESSIVE LANGUAGE

This test assesses the child's oral ability to express ideas in words. The ideas are grouped into 8 categories:

1. name of object or class to which the object belongs
2. colour
3. shape
4. composition
5. function, or action
6. characteristics
7. comparison

The focus is on the quantity of concepts a child has at his command, not on the quality of expression.

Material:

Test Item - The red, white and blue ball.

Procedure:

The child is shown the ball and asked to describe the ball verbally.

(a) He or she is encouraged to respond spontaneously with the instruction, "TELL ME ALL ABOUT THIS."

When and if he or she hesitates or appears reluctant, statements such as "TELL ME MORE ABOUT IT", or, "TELL ME SOME OTHER THINGS", are made.

If the child repeats the same idea, say, "YES, YOU TOLD ME ABOUT THAT. NOW TELL ME SOMETHING ELSE."

(b) When the child indicates he or she has nothing more to say, he or she is asked <u>direct questions</u> to determine what additional concepts are actually known but are not expressed spontaneously. The directed questions for each item are listed.

1. WHAT IS THIS CALLED? (Name)

2. WHAT COLOUR IS IT? (Colour)

3. WHAT SHAPE IS IT? (Shape)

4. WHAT IS IT MADE OF? (Composition)

5. WHAT DO YOU DO WITH IT? (Action or Function)

6. HOW DOES IT FEEL WHEN YOU TOUCH IT? (Characteristics)

7. CAN YOU THINK OF ANYTHING THAT LOOKS LIKE A BALL? (Comparison) (accept up to 6 responses)

Scoring Guide:

Ball	Responses
1. Name	Ball
2. Colour	Red, white, and blue (all three required)
3. Shape	round, circle
4. Composition	rubber
5. Function or action	Play with it or play baseball or play basketball, etc. Bounce, catch, hit, kick, chase, roll, throw.
6. Characteristics	hard solid, not hollow smooth spongy not heavy, light
7. Comparison	Some acceptable responses are: sun, apple, orange, marble, ball of dough, doll's head, teddy's head, balloon, pom pom (accept up to 6 objects which must be spherical).

Scoring:

Write the pupil's responses for the ball either under spontaneous or directed responses, then check the number of responses in each category in the appropriate spaces provided on the Pupil's Record Sheet.

Follow the scoring guide in crediting responses. Possible responses are separated into categories. Under each of these 8 categories responses specific to each are grouped so that similar responses will not receive double credit. Each creditable response, or group of similar responses are indicated by a capital letter.

    Credit 1 point for each <u>spontaneous response.</u>
    Credit 1 point for each <u>directed response</u>.

Record total points for Expressive Language. If no points are obtained, score as 0.

Each capitalized response can be credited with a point.

Rating Scale:

Rate the child on a scale of 0 to 5 using the following guide:

No. of Points	Scaled Score
0	0
1	1
2-3	2
4-5	3
6-9	4
10+	5

MATHEMATICAL SKILLS

Column 10

These skills indicate the child's ability to learn and to use number concepts.

Materials:

    20 blocks
    number symbol card

Procedure:

Place the above materials on the table.

1. Say: "COUNT FOR ME." If the child reaches 10, say, "STOP". Then ask him or her to count the following short sequences, beginning and ending as directed.

Say: "COUNT FROM 15 TO 25."

2. Put the blocks in a line. Point to the blocks and say: "COUNT THE BLOCKS FOR ME."

3. Say: "GIVE ME 2 BLOCKS, 4 BLOCKS, 7 BLOCKS, 10 BLOCKS, 12 BLOCKS."

4. Say: "I PUT 2 BLOCKS ON MY PAPER. YOU PUT MORE THAN 2 BLOCKS ON YOUR PAPER."

    "I PUT 4 BLOCKS ON MY PAPER. YOU PUT 1 MORE THAN 4 BLOCKS ON YOUR PAPER."

    "I PUT 3 BLOCKS ON MY PAPER. YOU PUT LESS THAN 3 BLOCKS ON YOUR PAPER."

    "I PUT 5 BLOCKS ON MY PAPER. YOU PUT 1 LESS THAN 5 BLOCKS ON YOUR PAPER."

If it is evident that the child is merely copying the demonstration, do not administer item 5, as it would have no validity.

5. Say: "I PUT 2 BLOCKS ON MY PAPER. YOU PUT THE SAME NUMBER OF BLOCKS ON YOUR PAPER.

    I PUT 5 BLOCKS ON MY PAPER. YOU PUT AN EQUAL NUMBER OF BLOCKS ON YOUR PAPER.

    I PUT 4 BLOCKS ON MY PAPER. YOU PUT NOT THE SAME NUMBER OF BLOCKS ON YOUR PAPER.

    I PUT 3 BLOCKS ON MY PAPER. YOU PUT AN UNEQUAL NUMBER OF BLOCKS ON YOUR PAPER.

6. Place the number card in front of the child. Point to the symbols and say: "WHAT DOES THIS NUMBER SAY?"

7. Say: "WHAT NUMBER COMES BEFORE 5?"

    "WHAT NUMBER COMES AFTER 7?"

    "WHAT NUMBER COMES BEFORE 10?"

    "WHAT NUMBER COMES AFTER 12?"

8. Present the following problems orally:

    "NANCY ATE 3 COOKIES. BOBBY ATE 2 COOKIES. HOW MANY COOKIES DID THEY EAT TOGETHER?"

    "MOTHER PUT 4 COOKIES ON A PLATE. BILLY ATE 1 COOKIE. HOW MANY COOKIES ARE LEFT?"

Scoring:

Score 1 point for each item passed on the Pupil's Record Sheet. Record the total number of points.

Rating Scale:

    Rate the child on a scale of 0 to 5 using the following guide:

No. of Points	Scaled Score
0	0
1-3	1
4-8	2
9-15	3
16-20	4
21+	5

Evaluation Scale for Teacher Use:

Please rate each child according to your estimation of his or her possible success in school subjects in the elementary grades.

    Likely to do very well _____

    Likely to do somewhat well _____

    Likely to be about average in performance _____

    Likely to have some difficulty _____

    Likely to have great difficulty _____

Appendix II

Report of the Consultant to the W.E.I.P., Part II

In the morning of Tuesday, January 23, discussions were held with Miss Erickson, Miss Elaine Cline, Primary Consultant, and Mr. Rick Gelinas of the Board's Computer Services.

From these discussions it was learned that a continuous record of academic achievement was begun in 1974 for 504 students entering the Kindergartens of 16 schools in September of that year. The record began with the results of the Kindergarten educational assessment, considered at that time to be statistically reliable. This was followed in later grades to the end of Grade 3 in June 1978 by the administration of tests based upon the curriculum in each grade. The content of these tests would be available through Miss Erickson.

The placement of students from Kindergarten and later grades for a following year was decided mainly on the results of the academic testing. Students who entered Grade 4 were given the Gates-MacGinitie test. The contents of this test and the results are also obtainable from Miss Erickson. A record of speech problems is also available.

In the course of the years from September 1974 to June 1978, a number of students have moved to different schools of the Windsor Board and some 25 have left this system. Records for students still in the schools of the Windsor Board should be available.

In the afternoon of January 23 discussions were held with Miss Erickson and two consultants in Special Education, Mrs. Virginia Benton and Mr. Maurice Van Mecklenberg, concerning students referred to Special Education over the four year period, 1974-78.

From a previous review of these referrals it was determined that 37 of the 504 students had been referred to Special Education for one reason or another. Thirty-two of these students were identified in Kindergarten as having some degree of academic need. Nine students with severe problems were referred from Kindergarten. The others were given further attention in the classroom with some benefit, but 8 in Reading Readiness and 15 in Grade 1 required further assistance and were referred from these grades.

Five students were referred to Special Education from Grade 2. Four of these had shown marked reversal tendencies and the classroom teacher sought additional advice.

One of the total of 37 students left this school system. Nine were placed in the Primary opportunity classes. One is in a Special School with a residential program. Twenty-six students are all in regular classes: five of them are in Grade 2, thirteen are in Grade 3, and eight are in Grade 4 (as of 1978).

Eight students placed in the Primary opportunity program are said to have made slow but upward progress; one has advanced to a Junior opportunity program. The details concerning these students are now being prepared by Mrs. Benton and Mr. Van Mecklenberg and should be available by mid February.

In the morning, afternoon, and evening of January 24 interviews were held with Dr. J. Jones, M.O.H., of the Metro Windsor-Essex County Health Unit and with Dr. George Fraser, a paediatrician who was a member on the Committee of the Windsor Early Identification Project. The discussion centred around the identification of problems that might affect learning in children younger than regular Kindergarten and also the question of the possible effect on the learning capability of children with birth weights of less than 5 lb. 8 oz.

The Health History form of the W.E.I.P. includes general questions about the pregnancy, the birth weight, and any complications for the infant (prematurity, one of twins, incubation therapy, etc.), and about the remembered stages of development. The mother of the child entering Kindergarten provided such information.

The adaptation of the Windsor program for Kindergarten identification to the Junior Kindergarten level has been considered. The procedures of parent involvement, the taking of the social and health histories, the testing of hearing and vision, and the recognition of organic speech problems could certainly be undertaken with benefit. However, there is concern about the method that might be used to determine learning capability at this age. Very careful consideration needs to be given to the type of assessment for knowledge of colour, receptive and expressive language, and number concepts. Should the foregoing be developed, then consideration should be given to an upgrading of the Kindergarten assessment.

The present Kindergarten educational assessment has been very satisfactory and its use in other school boards does not seem to require adjustments in scaled scores as indicated in my report to the Ministry of Education on the 1976 implementation elsewhere in Ontario. However, both Miss Erickson and Miss Cline would like to see an improvement in the Math area and some minor changes in the guidelines for the teacher in the Manual of Procedures.

Annotated Bibliography

Atkinson, Catherine Nelson. "The Effectiveness of Selected Case-Finding Approaches in Locating Handicapped Individuals Residing in Areas with Specified Demographic Characteristics." North Texas State University, 1977.

Conducted in the seven constituent counties of Region One Education Service Center of Texas, the study reviewed data from the first 4½ months of the identification phase of Project Child Find. It was found that the house to house canvass was the most effective case finding approach, followed by television.

Bach, Phillip Wendell. "The Efficacy of a Theory Based Screening Battery for the Identification and Classification of Underachieving Children in the Early Elementary Grades." Purdue University, 1975.

It was concluded from administration of the Metropolitan Achievement Tests, Primary II, Form F, and a battery of five tests of cognitive processes to 96 second grade children that the relationship between scores in the verbal and nonverbal portions of the battery may have utility in providing economical screening and preliminary diagnosis of patterns of underachievement.

Bechtel, Leland P. "The Detection and Remediation of Learning Disabilities." Androscoggin County Task Force on Social Welfare, Inc., Lewiston, Maine, 1975.

Reported are the final two years of a program which provided identification and remediation services for 60 potentially dyslexic preschool children and 45 dyslexic elementary grade children. Described for the preschool program are materials and evaluative devices and methods of remediation which stressed development of perceptual motor skills, applied skills, gross motor skills, and free play. Detailed are findings showing that the experimental group made 44 positive gains (out of 50 possible test scores) over the control group, 27 of which were significant (especially in such areas as the Wechsler full scale IQ, letter discrimination, word discrimination, copying and figure ground perception). It is explained that methods of remediation in the 6-week program for elementary grade dyslexic students included daily instruction in reading, perceptual motor skills, gross motor skills, English composition, and mathematics, as well as weekly field trips. Reported are conclusions showing that experimental students gained significantly over control students in such areas as figure ground perception, arithmetic computation, reading accuracy, and visual tracking. An additional section provides subjective observations and interpretations on such program aspects as teacher qualities, pupil attitudes, test anxiety and overloading, self esteem, professional and public awareness, and problems such as failure to mainstream pupils properly.

Becker, Laurence C. "Conceptual Tempo and the Early Detection of Learning Problems." Journal of Learning Disabilities. Vol. 9, No. 7 (August/September 1976), pp. 433-442.

The importance of regulation of conceptual tempo as a dimension of educational risk for identification of children with learning problems was investigated with 60 kindergarten children. Risk and nonrisk children (selected on the basis of behavioral observation and teacher ratings) were compared for impulsivity and ability to regulate tempo in situations of varying levels of task complexity and under varying sets of instructions. Results suggested that risk children were more impulsive than nonrisk children, and were also less able to alter tempo when going from simple to complex situations and when told to work fast or to work slow.

Bell, Anne E., et al. "Reading Retardation: A 12-Year Perspective Study." Journal of Pediatrics. Vol. 91, No. 3 (September 1977), pp. 363-370.

A 12-year longitudinal study involving almost 1,000 kindergarten children including normal and learning disabled students was conducted to assess the predictive efficiency of a preschool test battery in relation to short and long term school achievement, to evaluate socioeconomic locale and operational school structure as indicators of subsequent progress, and to observe the effects of some correctional experience on later school performance. Among findings were that 23% failed to complete first grade requirements in the first year; that failure rates within separate schools ranged from 3% to 71% and had an inverse relationship to socioeconomic level; and that within the middle class area, children in an open space school had double the failure rate of their peers in traditional classrooms.

Bone, Jan. "Peotone Fights School Failure." *American Education*. Vol. 13, No. 1 (January/February, 1977), pp. 32-35.

Early Prevention of School Failure is a low cost program in which children from 12 Illinois school districts are screened for learning disabilities before entering kindergarten and placed accordingly. Key components of the program are the screening, special classes, professional monitoring of children with special needs in regular classes, and consultative services for teachers. Parental assistance in the classroom is solicited actively. Teachers and assistants in special classes provide remediation in the areas of speech, language, audition, vision, motor ability, and social and emotional development. In 3 years, respectively 37, 63 and 68 percent of the learning disabled kindergarten children have been mainstreamed into regular classes.

Boothman, Rosemary, et al. "Predictive Value of Early Developmental Examination." *Archives of Disease in Childhood*. Vol. 51, No. 6 (June 1976), pp. 430-434.

To test the predictive value of early screening tests, a developmental examination was carried out on 168 children at the age of 4 weeks, 16 weeks, 28 weeks and 52 weeks, with a followup examination at 3 years of age. The results suggested that developmental screening of this type is effective in picking out the 'poor performers' who might well benefit from preschool education and extra health visitor supervision. On the other hand, the test given to children under the age of one year failed to pick out two children who were found to be moderately handicapped at the time of the 3-year examination.

Brenton, Beatrice White, and Gilmore, Doug. "An Operational Definition of Learning Disabilities (Cognitive Domain) Using WISC Full Scale IQ and Peabody Individual Achievement Test Scores." *Psychology in the Schools*. Vol. 13, No. 4 (October 1976), pp. 427-432.

Developed and tested with 50 male and 10 female elementary school students (6 to 13 years old) who were legally identified as learning disabled was an index of discrepancy to assist in determining an operational definition of learning disabilities in the cognitive domain. The index, derived from the Full Scale IQ score of the Wechsler Intelligence Scale for Children and relevant subtest scores on the Peabody Individual Achievement Test, identified 74% of the male subjects and 30% of the female subjects as possibly learning disabled in the cognitive domain.

Brown, Don A. "What Are the Issues?" <u>Sight-Saving Review</u>. Vol. 46, No. 2 (Summer 1976), pp. 59-63.

    Intended for those concerned with the identification of learning disabilities that involve communicative disorders, the article identifies some areas of confusion regarding visual perception, vision testing, communication, and dyslexia. It is suggested that evaluations be given in behavioral descriptive terms.

Bunner, Richard T. "Ohio's Comprehensive Vision Project." <u>Sight-Saving Review</u>. Vol. 43, No. 2 (Summer 1973).

    A vision screening program in seven Ohio counties tested 3,261 preschool children and 44,885 school age children for problems of distance visual acuity, muscle balance, and observable eye problems. Criteria were established for testing procedures and referrals. Forty-two percent of the estimated preschool population was tested with 205 children referred for further testing. Follow-up investigations revealed that over 90% of the referred children had received eye examinations and treatment. Only first grade children were tested for hyperopia, and 33 of the 95 children referred would not have received treatment had they only been tested for visual acuity.

Cohen, Marilyn Aronin. <u>Teacher Judgment Concerning Arithmetic Disabilities as Accounted for by a Functional Assessment Battery</u>. University of Washington, 1975.

    In the study involving 51 third graders, results showing that teacher judgment concerning arithmetic disabilities could be accounted for by a functional assessment battery indicated that discriminant analysis may be a useful technique for those seeking functional definitions of learning disabilities.

Colligan, Robert C. "Concurrent Validity of the Myklebust Pupil Rating Scale in a Kindergarten Population." <u>Journal of Learning Disabilities</u>. Vol. 10, No. 5 (May 1977), pp. 317-320.

    To determine the value of the Pupil Rating Scale in identifying children at risk for learning difficulty, a sample of 60 kindergarten children was studied intensively to determine whether the Pupil Rating Scale would correlate as well with achievement measures as reported in H. Myklebust's normative sample. The study included one group test designed to measure general learning readiness (Metropolitan Readiness Test), a group test more clearly tied to specific mastery of prereading tasks (Lippincott Reading Readiness Test), and individual assessment of each child's knowledge of letters and numbers. The significant correlations with these measures of outcome provide considerable support for the use of the Pupil Rating Scale in a kindergarten population.

Currie, Winifred. "Proposing a Model Assessment and Intervention Program for Learning Disabled Adolescents in a Typical School Population." Paper presented at the International Federation of Learning Disabilities (Second international scientific conference, Brussels, Belgium, January 3-7, 1975).

Reported are results of screening over 1,000 eighth or ninth grade students for learning disabilities, and suggested is an intervention program utilizing available local resources. The Currie-Milonas Screening Test is described as consisting of eight subtests to identify problems in the basic skills of reading, writing, language, or mathematics. Results indicated that 19.8% of eighth graders, 18.1% of ninth graders, and 28% of vocational education ninth graders were reading at the fourth grade level or below. Proposed is an intervention program involving classroom teachers, reading teachers, remedial reading specialists, supplemental clinical tutorial services, or referral to special day or residential schools.

Danhauer, Jeffrey L., and Singh, Sadanand. "A Cross Language Study of Speech Production of Children in Audio and Audio-Visual Modalities." *Acta Symbolica*. Vol. 4, No. 2 (Fall 1973), pp. 29-45.

Twenty logatomes involving five vowels and 20 consonants (in combinations such as "baba") were presented to 18 hard of hearing and 18 deaf speakers of English (American), Serbo-Croatian (Yugoslavian), and French, mean age 8-3/4 years. Results indicated that there were significant differences between deviancy groups, vowels, and consonants, and modalities (audio versus audio-visual); that no significant differences were found for three different low frequency amplication hearing aids and positions of initial and medial consonants, or medial and final vowels; and that significant correlations were found for the phonetic transcriptions of vowels and consonants independently, and for the overall rating scale judgements of the logatomes.

Davis, William E. "A Comparison of Teacher Referral and Pupil Self-Referral Measures Relative to Perceived School Adjustment." Paper presented at the Annual International Convention, the Council for Exceptional Children. Chicago, Illinois, April 4-9, 1976.

Investigated was the relationship between the perceived school adjustment of 215 female and 202 male fourth grade pupils and their classroom teachers' ratings in this area. Examined were the extent of teacher/pupil agreement relative to perceived learning and/or adjustment problems and the relationship between teacher referral or pupil self referral to sex of the child and type of problem indicated. A significant relationship was found between teacher referral and pupil self referral. However, a disproportionate number of male students were referred by their teachers (38% to 12%) and a much higher percentage of females (33%) referred themselves. Results suggested the need to include a pupil self referral component within the screening mechanism for the identification of children in need of special education services.

Doehring, Donald G., and Swisher, Linda P. "Tone Decay and Hearing Threshold Level in Sensorineural Loss." *Journal of Speech and Hearing Research*. Vol. 14, No. 2 (June 1971), pp. 345-349.

Tone decay was assessed by the Bekesy and modified Rosenberg procedures in audiological patients with sensorineural-type loss for whom there was no neurological evidence of retrocochlear pathology. Thirty-five subjects were tested at 500 Hz, 97 at 2000 Hz and 92 at 4000 Hz. Tone decay tended to increase with increased hearing threshold level for both tests at all three frequencies, with low but significant correlations at two of the three frequencies for each test. There were no systematic differences between the Bekesy and modified Rosenberg procedures with regard to overall level, frequency effects, or hearing threshold effects. A low but significant correlation was obtained between the two procedures at all three frequencies.

Evans, Joyce S. *A Project to Develop Curriculum for Four-Year-Old Handicapped Mexican American Children*. Vol. 1 of 2 volumes. Southwest Educational Development Lab., Austin, Texas, November 1974.

As part of the Ability Development Project to identify 4-year-old Mexican American children with learning disabilities and develop appropriate curricular materials for them, 99 children (3-5 years old) attending city day care centers were assigned to the Bilingual Early Childhood Program, Level II. Twenty-nine children (final results included data on only 22 of this group) identified by Project staff as having the most severe learning disabilities were selected as the target population. Identification instruments and supplementary activities were developed or adapted using a pre-post test research design that compared results from the target group with results from nonhandicapped classmates and handicapped children who had not received supplementary assistance. The following products resulted: Spanish/English Language Preference Screening, Observational Checklists for Referral, Criterion Referenced Test, Supplementary Activities, the Instructional Materials Manual, "How to Fill Your Toy Shelves Without Emptying Your Pocketbook--70 Inexpensive Things to Do or Make", and a manual on working with parents of handicapped children. Findings included that project children made significant gains on criterion referenced and norm referenced tests; and that target children who had received Supplementary Activities made greater gains than target children who had not, and in some areas made gains comparable with those of their nonhandicapped peers.

Evans, Joyce. <u>Identification and Supplementary Instruction for Handicapped Children in a Regular Bilingual Program</u>. Southwest Educational Development Laboratory, Austin, Texas, 1976.

The Ability Development Projects were designed to identify the preschool Mexican American child with existing and/or potentially handicapping conditions, to develop and test supplementary materials and to determine the efficacy of supplementary instruction within the regular bilingual classroom. In the first project for 4-year-olds, 40 out of 99 children enrolled had some type of problem, 29 children with problems severe enough to interfere with learning. Following 5 months of supplementary instruction, the experimental group out-performed the comparison group not receiving supplementary instruction and were learning at the level of nonhandicapped peers. In the second project for 5-year-olds, materials for continuous observation and supplementary instruction on a lesson-by-lesson basis were developed which include two identification instruments, the Spanish/English Language Performance Screening and the Observational Checklists for Referral, and four instructional materials, Working with Parents of Handicapped Children, How to Fill Your Toy Shelves Without Emptying Your Pocketbook, Supplementary Activities for Four-Year-Olds and Observation-Activity Cards for Five-Year-Olds.

Federici, Louise, et al. "Use of the Meeting Street School Screening Test and the Myklebust Pupil Rating Scale with First-Grade Black Urban Children." *Psychology in the Schools*. Vol. 13, No. 4 (October 1976), pp. 386-389.

Tested with 580 first grade urban Black subjects was the use of the Meeting Street School Screening Test (MSSST) and the Myklebust Pupil Rating Scale for the early identification of children with potential learning problems. Results supported the use of the tests with this population in that (1) the MSSST identified the same proportion (15%) of high risk subjects in the experimental group that is estimated for the general population, (2) the Myklebust discriminated between high risk (N=22) and low risk (N=21) subjects within the minority group using the MSSST as the criterion variable, and (3) Myklebust ratings for the subjects approximated ratings reported elsewhere for older White suburban subjects.

Findlay, Robert C. "Auditory Dysfunction Accompanying Noise-Induced Hearing Loss." *Journal of Speech and Hearing Disorders*. Vol. 41, No. 3 (August 1976).

Auditory dysfunction accompanying noise induced hearing loss was examined with 16 male subjects (18 to 29 years old) who had 12- to 24-month histories of noise exposure and high frequency hearing loss. Speech discrimination test scores indicated that before significant hearing loss is apparent at the midfrequencies, speech perception difficulties may occur under conditions of competing speech and noise. Comparison of subjects with a control group indicated that tests of the basic audiometric battery may not indicate the full extent of auditory dysfunction related to noise induced hearing loss.

Fisher, Lee I. "Efficiency and Effectiveness of Using a Portable Audiometric Booth in School Hearing Conservation Programs." *Language, Speech, and Hearing Services in Schools*. Vol. 7, No. 4 (October 1976), pp. 242-249.

Investigated was the efficiency and effectiveness of using a portable sound treated booth in detecting hearing impairments during screening of 350 children (kindergarten-grade 6) in a public school hearing conservation program. The subjects, who were first screened in an open environment and in a portable audiometric booth, were then given a threshold test in an audiometric sound treated booth in a portable van with audiometers calibrated to standards set by the American National Standards Institute. Results indicated that there was a significant benefit in using a portable sound treated enclosure during the initial screening to correctly identify larger percentages of students with or without hearing impairment; the major value being the reduction of wasted time spent in retesting students with normal hearing.

Forness, Steven, et al. "Follow-Up of High-Risk Children Identified in Kindergarten Through Direct Classroom Observation." Psychology in the Schools. Vol. 13, No. 1 (January 1976), pp. 45-49.

From a prior kindergarten population sample, 61 first grade students were involved in a follow-up study to determine the validity of observable classroom behaviour evaluations in predicting educational risk. Teacher ratings and individual achievement test scores at follow-up for the children originally classified into four behavioural clusters (ranking risk) showed that the nonrisk cluster continued to do well, while high risk children were doing poorly in some areas; and that children in a cluster originally viewed as nonrisk were also having difficulty in school.

Frankenburg, William K., et al. "Implications of Early Screening for Later Development." Final Report, July 1, 1974 - February 26, 1976. Colorado University, Denver, Medical Centre.

Presented is a letter regarding the final report of a project involving the follow up of 151 children (under 6 years old at the time of the initial assessment) to establish the accuracy of the Denver Developmental Screening Test in predicting school achievement problems. Reviewed are the procedures used in selecting the study population, and explained are changes made in the proposal regarding the follow up assessments.

Gerwin, Kenneth S., and Glorig, Aram (eds.) Detection of Hearing Loss and Ear Disease in Children. (Springfield, Ill.: Charles C. Thomas, 1974).

Intended for otolaryngologists, pediatricians, audiologists, and school nurses, the book provides 20 author-contributed chapters on ear disease, the detection of hearing loss, and the Callier study which involved examining 811 4-year-old children for hearing loss and ear disease. Papers on the background of ear disease and hearing loss detection have the following titles and authors: "Auditory

Deprivation and Learning" (J. Stewart), "Review of Literature for Causes of Ear Disease in Children" (K. Gerwin), "Identification Audiometry" (R. Hood and L. Lamb), "Hearing Conservation" (A. Glorig and K. Gerwin), "Background of Verbal Auditory Screening for Children" (B. Ritchie), "Review of the Literature--Verbal Auditory Screening for Children" (B. Ritchie). The Callier Study is reported in the following papers: "Introduction, Protocol, and Data Collection Forms" (K. Gerwin), "Selection of Subjects and Audiology" (N. Goode), "Otological Examination" (K. Gerwin), "Some Thoughts on Statistical Analysis" (C. Read), "Verbal Auditory Screening for Children" (A. Glorig), "Use of Medical Questionnaire to Identify Hearing Loss" (K. Gerwin and C. Read), "The Medical History in Identifying Hearing Loss" (K. Gerwin and C. Read), "Pure Tone Sweepcheck as an Indicator of the Pure Tone Threshold Test" (A. Glorig), "The Pure Tone Threshold Test" (A. Glorig), "Ear Pathology and Hearing Loss" (K. Gerwin and C. Read), "Physical Characteristics that are Possible Predisposing Causes of Ear Disease and Hearing Loss" (K. Gerwin and C. Read), "Causes of Ear Disease in the Callier Study" (K. Gerwin and C. Read), "Comparison of the Screening Tests with the Diagnostic Studies" (K. Gerwin), and "Summary and Recommendations" (K. Gerwin and A. Glorig).

Givens, Gregg, D., and Seidemann, Michael F. "Middle Ear Measurements in a Difficult to Test Mentally Retarded Population." *Mental Retardation*. Vol. 15 (October 1977), pp. 40-42.

Thirty-eight mentally retarded persons who failed audiometric screening at school were evaluated tympanometrically. Results indicated extremely high incidence of abnormal middle ear pressure and/or function. Few subjects were nontestable, though all had IQs less than 35.

Gouge, Betty Merle Gage. *A Reliability and Validity Study of the VADS Test for Screening Learning Disabilities of Second Graders With Teachers as Examiners.* Texas Woman's University, 1975.

Evaluated with 460 second grade classrooms was E. Koppitz's Visual-Aural Digit Span (VADS) Test which measures short term memory and intra- and intersensory integration. Results indicated that the VADS yielded highly reliable results with validity correlations all positive and significant ranging from low to high correlations.

Grassi, Fay Ruth. Predicting Special Class Placement of Elementary School Pupils with the Use of the Burks' Behavior Rating Scale. University of Northern Colorado, 1976.

Results of the study in which teachers completed the Burks' Behavior Rating Scale for 315 students referred for learning and/or behavior problems indicated that the measure had low probabilities of predicting particular special education placements except for the severe oral language handicapped/ aphasia pupils. The measure did predict, however, whether girls in grades 1 through 3 and all elementary school boys would be referred for regular or special class placement.

Hollinshead, Merrill T. "Pre-School Program for Emotionally Disturbed, Language and Perceptually Impaired Children (Title VI) Evaluation Period (December 1974 - June 1975). Evaluation Report." New York City Board of Education, Brooklyn, N.Y., Office of Educational Evaluation, 1975.

Evaluated was a program designed to make an early diagnosis of the emotional problems and learning disabilities of 40 preschool children, and to furnish educational interventions so that these problems might be ameliorated before the children enter formal schooling. The program centered around speech and language, perceptual motor activities and adjustment to peers and adults. Evaluation objectives in areas of language, perceptual motor development, social and emotional behaviour, and attitudes toward and relationships with adults in the educational setting. Pre- and post-test data revealed that statistically significant differences in the direction of gains and improvement were obtained. There was also close agreement between staff members that over 75% of the children had improved moderately or markedly in attitudes toward and relationships with adults. (Among appended materials are statistical data and a sample form used to collect ratings of improvement.)

Hull, Raymond H. "Groups vs. Individual Screening in Public School Audiometry." Colorado Journal of Educational Research. Vol. 13, No. 1 (1973), pp. 6-9.

Evaluated with 5,108 school children were differences between individual pure-tone audiometric screening and group (10 children at a time) pure-tone audiometric screening. Of the students given the individual screening, 48.6% were found to be over-referrals (without a hearing loss), while 31.7% of the students given the group screening were found to be over-referrals. Findings suggested that the speed and efficiency of the group screening technique combined with the lowered percent of over-referrals indicates the group method to be more efficient than the individual method.

Jacobs, Jacqueline E., and Sacatsh, Jean. "Kindergarten Diagnostic Assessment of Learning Style." Paper presented at the International Scientific Federation of Learning Disabilities (Second International Scientific Conference, Brussels, Belgium, January 3-7, 1975).

Described is a program to identify potential learning problems and learning styles in 131 kindergarten children through the assessment of global intelligence, gross and fine motor skills, visual perception skills, auditory perception skills, speech and language development, social skills, alphabet recognition, and number concepts. Standardized tests and informal assessment measures used in the screening program are described. It is explained that organization of the testing program involves eight testing stations; a professional staff of three social workers, two psychologists, three speech therapists, and one learning disabilities teacher; and 20 volunteer parents or graduate students. It is reported that the program has distinguished five groups of children ranging from children needing gross motor or language experiences to children ready for the pre-reading program.

Johnson, E.W. "Let's Look at the Child Not the Audiogram." Volta Review, Vol. 69. Washington: Alexander Graham Bell Association for Deaf, 1967.

Case reports of three aurally handicapped children are presented to show the importance of not labeling a child deaf or hard of hearing on the basis of his audiogram alone. Although the three children had severe hearing losses, they were capable of adjusting to a hard of hearing school program and were doing well. Because of their audiogram results, two were transferred to a deaf program and then regressed in school work and motivation. The third student was doing well in a school for normal hearing high school students, though her audiogram classified her as profoundly deaf. Conclusions show that different children respond differently to hearing aids. Some children use residual hearing to function as hard of hearing in spite of an audiogram indicating deafness, while others may function as normal hearing children when the audiogram indicates hearing loss (in the hard of hearing range). It is recommended that parents, audiologists, clinicians, and teachers of the deaf determine how the youngster functions and not depend on the audiogram results.

Jones, R. Wayne. The Target Groups: Description of Learning Disabled and Normal Subjects Participating in Prototype Evaluation Studies. Georgia State University, Atlanta, 1975.

Compared were the characteristics of 60 learning disabled and 60 normal children (all between 8 and 11 years old) participating in the Georgia Reading Research Program. The target group consisted of learning disabled children who showed deficits in the psychological process of ordering/sequencing, while the learning disabled reference group was average or above average in ordering/sequencing abilities. Instruments used to assess these deficits were the Wechsler Intelligence Scale for Children Sequencing Triad and the Wide Range Achievement Spelling Test. Other differences between the two groups were that the target group had instructional reading levels 1 or more years below their expected grade placement levels and were enrolled in special classes; while the learning disabled reference children were enrolled in regular classes and were reading within 6 months of expected grade level. The program focussed on an evaluation of specific curriculum treatments designed to facilitate reading achievement.

Kealy, Jean, and McLeod, John. "Learning Disability and Socioeconomic Status." Journal of Learning Disabilities. Vol. 9, No. 9 (November 1976), pp. 596-599.

Investigated with 333 children in grades 4 and 6 of three western Canadian urban public schools was the relationship between diagnosis of learning disabilities and socioeconomic status. Of the 35 subjects defined as learning disabled (18 from families with socioeconomic status above the median and 17 from below the median) 13 of the upper socioeconomic status group (72.5%) had been diagnosed by the Pupil Services Department, whereas only 5 (35.2%) of the lower socioeconomic status group had been diagnosed.

Kirschenbaum, Daniel S., et al. "The Effectiveness of a Mass Screening Procedure in an Early Intervention Program." Psychology in the Schools. Vol. 14, No. 4 (October 1977), pp. 400-406.

The effectiveness of a mass screening procedure (which consisted primarily of teachers rating the frequency of all primary grade children's acting out, moody withdrawal, and learning problem behaviours) was examined within the context of a preventively oriented school based treatment program in three inner city schools. While teachers directly referred 6.9% of the primary grade population, mass screening subsequently identified an additional 9.7%. Both referred and screened-in groups were rated by teachers on the Child Activity Rating Scale (CARS) as behaving less adaptively relative to a normative group. Referred children evidenced greatest overall dysfunctioning with most pronounced acting out and learning problems according to ratings by teachers. Further evidence of the validity of the CARS rating form was demonstrated by the agreement between staff predictions of CARS scores and actual ratings by teachers.

Lanier, Joe Harrison. <u>Cognitive Abilities Test Score Patterns for Possible Utilization in Identifying Children with Learning Disabilities</u>. Duke University, 1976.

A study involving 50 elementary students suspected of having learning disabilities and 50 control group students concluded that particular patterns on the Cognitive Abilities Test may be used to identify children with learning disabilities.

Larsen, Stephen C., et al. "The Use of Selected Perceptual Tests in Differentiating Between Normal and Learning Disabled Children." <u>Journal of Learning Disabilities</u>. Vol. 9, No. 2 (February, 1976), pp. 85-90.

Investigated was the diagnostic usefulness of commonly used tests of perceptual functioning with 30 normal and 59 learning disabled children (all 8-10 years old). Subjects were administered the Auditory and Visual Sequential Memory and Sound Blending subtests of the Illinois Test of Psycholinguistic Abilities, the Wepman Auditory Discrimination Test, and the Bender Visual Motor Gestalt Test. Statistical analyses revealed that only the Bender Visual Motor Gestalt Test differentiated the normal and learning disabled groups. Results suggested that continued use of these tests for purposes of diagnosis and placement should be reevaluated.

Levin, Susan, and Erber, Norman P. "A Vision Screening Program for Deaf Children." <u>Volta Review</u>. Vol. 78, No. 2 (February/March 1976), pp. 90-99.

A school-wide vision screening program was conducted at Central Institute for the Deaf to identify correctable and uncorrectable visual abnormalities in 165 children (4-16 years old). Another purpose of the screening program was to evaluate a variety of simple vision tests that could be administered by nonmedical personnel, in order to assemble a test battery appropriate for screening children with limited language. Tests of distant and near visual acuity, binocular vision (depth perception and fusion), colour vision, and peripheral vision were evaluated. Most of the tests were found to be useful in identifying visual deficiencies in hearing impaired children 4 years of age and older.

Loss, Barbara Lynn. <u>The Identification of Aptitude Describers Common to High-Risk Preschool Children with Potential Learning Problems</u>. Wayne State University, 1976.

In the study involving 389 preschool children, the following five variables were found to significantly discriminate high risk children: word knowledge, verbal memory-rote, sound blending, auditory reception, and quantitative (understanding of quantity concepts.)

Magliocca, L.A., et al. "Early identification of handicapped children through a frequency sampling technique." <u>Exceptional Children</u>. Vol. 43 (April 1977), pp. 414-420.

A pilot study was initiated with three regular preschool classes (65 children) to determine the validity of identifying preschool handicapped children (3½ to 5½ years of age) through a frequency sampling technique. The frequencies of correct responses of each child on the nine 1 minute academic tasks (e.g. matching colours) were counted. A list of at risk learners was developed consisting of all children performing in the lower 25% of frequency scores. Three conclusions emerged from the study: (1) the amount of instructional time saved through screening is critical; (2) teacher variables were not an issue in the screening; and (3) the predictive validity of screening through a frequency sampling technique is high.

Margolis, Howard. "The Kindergarten Auditory Screening Test as a Predictor of Reading Disability." <u>Psychology in the Schools</u>. Vol. 13, No. 4 (October 1976), pp. 399-403.

Examined with 93 kindergarten subjects was the use of the Kindergarten Auditory Screening Test (KAST) as an effective predictor of reading disability. Results from a comparison of correlation coefficients for the KAST with the Metropolitan Readiness Test given in kindergarten and the Gates MacGinitie Reading Tests (Primary Form) given in first grade indicated that the KAST was an inadequate screening device for the sample studied.

Merenda, Peter F., et al. "Identification Scale." *Psychology in the Schools*. Vol. 14, No. 3 (July 1977)

Described is a study involving 851 children in grades K through 2 to determine the reliability of the Rhode Island Pupil Identification Scale (RIPIS), a behaviour observation scale for identifying young children with learning problems. Detailed are analyses of data regarding internal consistency, stability of individual subscale scores, stability of Part I and Part II profiles, and homogeneity of Part I and Part II total scores. Results are said to indicate that all subscales, profiles, and composites were highly internally consistent and stable over a 5 month period.

Munns, Evangeline Francis. *The Development of a Teachers' Observation Scale for the Identification of Children with Learning Disabilities.* York University, 1971.

A 70 item scale covering classroom behaviour characteristics of children 6 to 13 years old with learning problems was developed and tested for construct validity with 287 children and for discriminant validity with 105 children. Results indicated that the scale was reliable for use by teachers as a screening tool.

Neel, Richard S. "A Psychometric Investigation of Identification of Children with Academic Difficulties." *Journal of Special Education*. Vol. 10, No. 1 (Spring 1976), pp. 91-95.

A group of 120 children with academic difficulties were studied to determine specific subpopulations by use of psychometric measures. The subjects, clinically identified as having academic difficulties, came from the Switzer Center for Educational Therapy and were selected by age (6-9) and IQ scores. Staff psychologists administered the Wechsler Intelligence Scale for Children, Illinois Test of Psycholinguistic Abilities, Frostig Developmental Test of Visual Perception, and Wepman Auditory Discrimination to subjects, who were then classified into groups according to certain variables. Their scores were factor analyzed to determine whether or not specific identifying variables could be determined. Four factors were found: intelligence, visual, language, and auditory. Performance and verbal scores on the WISC did not seem to differentiate specific subpopulations of children with academic difficulties.

Project OPEN 1974-1975 Child Service Demonstration Center
    Title VI - GC ESEA. Final Report. Brockton Public
    Schools, Mass., 1975.

   The final report of Project OPEN Child Service
   Demonstration Center, a program designed for identification and instruction of junior high learning
   disabled sutdents, summarizes project goals and
   achievements in screening methods, staff training,
   educational planning, and pupil performance.

Rogers, George W., and Richmond, Bert O. Results on the
    Slosson Drawing Coordination Test with Appalachian
    Sheltered Workshop Clients. 1975.

   Fifty-four clients (13 to 52 years old) in an
   Appalachian sheltered workshop were administered
   the Slosson Drawing Coordination Test (SDCT) and
   the Bender Visual Motor Gestalt test. Twenty-
   nine subjects were labelled possibly brain damaged
   by the SDCT, and 17 subjects by the M. Hutt scoring
   system for the Bender-Gestalt. Two psychologists
   using all available data and clinical judgment
   classified only 13 in a similar category. Results
   indicated the need for caution in using the SDCT
   as a screening instrument for brain damage among
   Appalachian clients.

Spalding, Norma Vivian Snyder. The Validation of a Neuro-
    logical Screening Test for Learning Disabilities.
    University of California at Berkeley, 1972.

   In a study to validate the effectiveness of the
   Quick Neurological Screening Test (QNST), comparing
   the performance of 88 elementary and high school
   children identified as learning disabled with 88
   matched controls, it was concluded that the QNST
   measured neurological signs which differentiate
   between learning disabled and normal children.

Spalding, Norma V., and Geiser, Marilyn Charlesworth. "Teacher
    Testing with the QNST." Academic Therapy. Vol. 13,
    No. 3 (January 1978), pp. 313-321.

   Four classroom teachers minimally trained to use the
   Quick Neurological Screening TEST (QNST) tested 13
   high achievers and 11 learning disabled elementary
   students. A significant correlation was found
   between the teachers' ratings and the ratings of
   four experts who had used the QNST extensively.
   The teachers were able, after minimal training,
   to identify the normal and the neurologically
   impaired students.

Stephens, M. Irene, and Daniloff, Raymond. "A Methodological Study of Factors Affecting the Judgment of Misarticulated s." Journal of Communications Disorders. Vol. 10, No. 3 (September 1977), pp. 207-220.

Described are two studies involving methods of judging misarticulated 's' in three kindergarten children who displayed clinically different 's' misarticulations, six specially chosen 's' defective subjects, and eight normally speaking subjects (aged from preschool to adult). Judgments in the first study were based on simultaneous audio and video recordings. Results indicated a large proportion of judgments in the questionable category, relatively low interjudge reliability, and few clear enhancing contexts. Judgments in the second study were made under live conditions and from tape recorded conditions. Results indicated the following: both normal and 's' defectives were easily and reliably detected under live speaking conditions, but were less easily detected from tape recordings; and, certain phonetic contexts, especially adjacent apical stops, appeared to encourage judgments of correct 's' misarticulations.

Sterling, Harold M., and Sterling, Patricia J. "Experiences with the QNST." Academic Therapy. Vol. 12, No. 3 (Spring 1977), pp. 339-342.

Described are preliminary findings from a study involving the use of the Quick Neurological Screening Test, the Denver Developmental Screening Test (DDST) and complete physical examinations for over 250 preschool and primary students. It is explained that the DDST identified only 17% of children found by physical examination to have organic neurological disorders, while 56% of children with neurological disorders successfully passed all four DDST subtests.

Sterling, Harold M., and Sterling, Patricia J. "Further Experiences with the QNST." Academic Therapy. Vol. 12, No. 4 (Summer 1977), pp. 487-490.

To investigate associations between vestibular function, balance, related neurodevelopmental, or neurophysiological test results and learning success or failure, each of 66 children with learning disorders was given an assessment which included the Quick Neurological Screening Test (QNST). Findings suggested an empirical relationship between QNST subtest results (particularly those relating to balance) and auditory receptive skills.

Taylor, Ian G. The Neurological Mechanisms of Hearing and Speech in Children. Manchester University Press, Washington.

A 5-year longitudinal study of 78 children (minimum age 11 months) who were referred to the Department of Deaf Education at the University of Manchester, England, is described. The children all presented problems related to sound or linguistic development or both. After a description of the physiology of hearing and the pathology of deafness, the methods and values of the electroencephalogram, the galvanic skin response, and behaviouristic tests of hearing are explained. Case histories are presented for peripherally deaf, aphasic and dysphasic, mentally defective, cerebral palsied, and visually handicapped children. Instructions for teachers and parental guidance are also covered. Results of the tests of hearing are presented. Photographs and figures illustrate the text. A bibliography lists 90 items.

Touwen, Bert C.L., et al. "Neurological Screening of Full-Term Newborn Infants." Developmental Medicine and Child Neurology. Vol. 19, No. 6 (December 1977), pp. 739-747.

To evaluate the reliability of H. Prechtl's "quick" (5 to 10 minute) screening procedure in selecting those infants who need a more comprehensive neurological examination, 100 full term newborn infants in a hospital were screened on the fourth or fifth day after birth. Of the 48 infants who as a result of the screening were then given the comprehensive examination, 25 showed definite deviant neurological signs; the other 23 proved normal. Four of the 52 infants screened as normal showed slight neurological deviations during the comprehensive assessment. These results underline the fact that neurological screening, while useful in selecting those infants who need further investigation, cannot replace a comprehensive examination. (Tables showing criteria for neurological optimality for full term newborn infants, and the distribution of diagnoses of neurological syndromes in relation to results on neurological screening, are included.)

Vance, Hubert (Booney), et al. "Analysis of Cognitive Abilities for Learning Disabled Children." Psychology in the Schools. Vol. 13, No. 4 (October 1976), pp. 477-483.

Studied with 58 learning disabled children (6 to 15 years old) was the use of differential Wechsler Intelligence Scale for Children-Revised subtest pattern scores in the diagnosis of learning disability. Analyses of the variation in subjects subtest scores indicated that the low subtest scores on Arithmetic,

Coding and Information were characteristic of this group. The study did not support the Verbal-Performance discrepancies as useful in the diagnosis of learning disabilities.

Van Doorninck, William J., et al. "Infant and Preschool Developmental Screening and Later School Performance." Paper presented at the Society for Pediatric Research, St. Louis, Missouri, April 1976.

A follow-up study of 151 lower socioeconomic class children (under 6 years of age at the time of initial screening) was conducted to determine the effectiveness of the Denver Developmental Screening Test (DDST) in predicting school achievement problems. Subjects were originally categorized into three age groups (0 to 2 years, 2 to 4 years, and 4 to 6 years) and three DDST classifications (normal, questionable, and abnormal). Follow-up evaluation (which took place when subjects' school placement ranged from beginning kindergarten to grade 5) included the following: achievement test percentiles, grade placement or special education status, and teacher ratings on the school Behaviour Check List. Based on the above data, subjects were classified as having school problems if they met one or more of four criteria (which included achievement test percentiles of 10 or less). Results indicated that the majority of subjects categorized as nonnormal had later school problems and that prediction became more accurate with increasing age of screening in abnormals.

<u>Vision and Hearing Screening in Selected Classes for the Mentally Retarded.</u> Michigan Department of Public Health, Detroit Children's Bureau, Welfare Administration, Washington.

To determine (1) whether routine screening procedures could be used successfully with retarded children and (2) the prevalence of uncorrected defects among a particular school population, retarded children from schools located in the lowest socioeconomic area of Detroit were screened for vision and hearing losses. Subjects' ages ranged from 3 to 21 years with a mean age of 12.6 years and their IQ's ranged from 30 to 75 with a mean IQ of 64. A total of 1,023 subjedts participated in the vision screening program and 688 subjects participated in the hearing screening program. Skilled technicians did the screening. The measures used were those standard for screening normal children. A stereoscopic instrument was used for most of the vision screening. Vision tests included were (1) for visual acuity, (2) a plus lens test, and (3) a muscle balance test. Hearing tests prepared a pure tone air conduction audiogram for each child using standard, commercially available screening audiometers. With both vision and hearing tests, a short orientation and preparation period preceded the test. Vision tests resulted in 30 percent referral, and hearing tests in a 7.2 percent referral. Results indicated that standard procedures can be used for screening vision and hearing in mentally retarded children from low income areas. The prevalence of previously undetected defects in both hearing and vision was found to be three times higher than in the general school population.

Wiener, Gerald. "The Bender Gestalt Test as a Predictor of Minimal Neurologic Deficit in Children Eight to Ten Years of Age." *Nervous and Mental Disease*. Vol. 143 (1966).

Designed to relate types of Bender-Gestalt impairment to minimal neurological deficit, this study gathered data about 417 premature and 405 full term children, aged 8 to 10, and matched according to race, sex, and economic status. Data were obtained from hospital records, mothers' reports, and a pediatric neurological evaluation neonatal history, and were applied to a nineteen-variable, unweighted scale used as an operational definition of minimal neurological deficit. Subjects were scored on the Wechsler Intelligence Scale for Children and the Bender-Gestalt variables with the neurologic deficit scale and the birth weight. Seven individual Bender-Gestalt variables correlated .22 with a scale score related to presumed minimal brain damage. Gross distortions and inability to produce angles and curves seemed to be significant independent predictions. The total Bender-Gestalt Score significantly discriminated between neurologic groups when the verbal IQ and race were controlled, and between neurologic groups for both White and Negro children.

Wilson, John D., et al. "Mission: Audition." *Journal of Special Education*. Vol. 10, No. 1 (Spring 1976), pp. 77-81.

Complete audiological evaluations were administered to 1482 children and adults enrolled at a residential and day center for persons with learning or adjustment problems to determine the number, type, and severity of hearing problems. Results indicated that 27.3% of this population had clinically significant hearing losses. Analysis of the data and related literature indicated that modifications in audiometric procedures in placement and programming decisions and in professional training should occur if exceptional learners, particularly those with multiple disabilities, are to receive maximally effective services.

Wold, Robert M. "The San Ysidro Study." Optometric Weekly. Vol. 62, No. 20 (May 1971), pp. 451-458.

    Described is a study conducted in San Ysidro, California, on the sight and vision capacity of minority/culturally deprived children. The screening project's purpose was to determine the visual needs of the community and to implement means of meeting these needs if their magnitudes were found to require it. Screened were 270 primarily Mexican-American children, grades pre-one through six. The screening program included these procedures: a developmental questionnaire completed by parents, an observation questionnaire completed by teachers, a comprehensive sight screening battery used for referrals, and vision screening tests (handedness, Winter Haven Copy Forms Test, and the Schilder Arm Extension Test). Clinical criteria for referral following closely those of the Modified Clinical Technique (MCT) are presented. Statistical data on refractive status, visual acuity, binocular eye coordination, eye health, and other test results are presented, and failure rates of the subjects on the various tests are compared. Among other results it is reported that 42.6% failed the MCT criteria; when professional judgment was added to the MCT scoring, 19.6% of the subjects failed the sight screening. Optometric services, including but not limited to vision screening, which should be included in a community health service center are proposed.

Young, Ellery, and Tracy, John M., III. "An Experimental Short Form of the Staggered Spondaic Word List for Learning Disabled Children." Audiology and Hearing Education. Vol. 3, No. 1 (December 1977), pp. 7-8, 10-11, 30.

    Investigated with 20 learning disabled children (between 7 and 11 years of age) was the use of a short form of the Staggered Spondaic Word List which uses speech audiometry in the presentation of a dichotic listening task for detection of central auditory impairment. Testing included pure tone test procedures, speech audiometric procedures, and the central auditory testing procedure in which the subject receives independent input in each ear. Results indicated that the learning disabled subjects had a significantly higher incidence of central auditory problems than the normal controls, and that the short form was as sensitive to the detection of central auditory dysfunction as the longer form.

Zahn, Thomas Paul. Identification of Sensory Motor and Perceptual Limitation. Potential Learning Disability and Hyperkinetic Behavior Disorder in Kindergarten Children. St. John's University, Jamaica, N.Y., 1975.

Among conclusions reached in the study involving 224 kindergarten children were that brief screening tests can be valid detectors of kindergarten children with perceptual and learning problems, and that the incidence of hyperkinesis in kindergarten children diminishes as the occurence of perceptual difficulty decreases.

Bibliography

"Activities Manual for Florida Language Profile." School Board of St. Lucie Country, Ft. Pierce, Florida. (Date unknown.)

Allen, K.E.; Rieke, J.; and Dmitriev, V. "Early warning: observation as a tool for recognizing potential handicaps in young children." Educational Horizons. Vol. 50 (Winter 1971-72), pp. 43-55.

Alston, H.L., and Doughtie, E.B. "Correspondence of constructs measured by the Kindergarten screening inventory by sex and ethnic group." Psychology in the Schools. Vol. 12 (October 1975), pp. 428-429.

Anderson, J. (ed.). Learning disabilities; diagnosis and treatment. Armidale, N.S.W., University of New England, 1971.

Anderson, M., et al. "Use of the WISC-R with a learning disabled population: some diagnostic implications." Psychology in the Schools. Vol. 13 (October 1976), pp. 381-386.

Asbed, R.A., et al. "Preschool Roundup: Costly rodeo or primary prevention?" Health Education. Vol. 8 (July/Aug. 1977), pp. 17-19.

Ashlock, Patrick, and Dolan, Mary. "The Saint Giles LD Identification Project." Paper presented at the International Scientific Conference of IFLD. Montreal, 1976.

Ashlock, Patrick, and Thompson, Glen. "The Ashlock Tests of Visual Perception." Revised. Paper presented at the International Scientific Conference of IFLD. Montreal, 1976.

Atkinson, Catherine Nelson. "The Effectiveness of Selected Case-Finding Approaches in Locating Handicapped Individuals Residing in Areas with Specified Demographic Characteristics." North Texas State University, 1977.

Auxter, D. "Perceptual motor characteristics of preschool children with suspected learning disabilities." Psychology in the Schools. Vol. 8 (April, 1971), pp. 148-151.

Bach, Phillip Wendell. "The Efficacy of a Theory Based Screening Battery for the Identification and Classification of Underachieving Children in the Early Elementary Grades." Purdue University, 1975.

Badian, N.A., and Serwer, B.L. "Identification of high risk children: A retrospective look at selection criteria." Journal of Learning Disabilities. Vol. 8 (May 1975), pp. 283-287.

Banas, Norma, and Wills, I.H. Identifying Early Learning Gaps: A Guide to the Assessment of Academic Readiness. (Atlanta: Humanic Press, 1975.)

Banas, Norma, and Wills, I.H. "Prescriptions from WISC-R Patterns." Academic Therapy. Vol. 13 (November, 1977), pp. 241-246.

Banks, E.M. "Identifying and helping the learning disabled child in the classroom." Independent Education. Vol. 4, No. 1 (February/March, 1975), pp. 10-18.

Bax, Martin C.O. "The Assessment of the Child at School Entry." Pediatrics. Vol. 58, No. 3 (September, 1976), pp. 403-407.

Beatty, J.R. "Analysis of an instrument for screening learning disabilities. Individual learning disabilities program classroom screening instrument." Journal of Learning Disabilities. Vol. 8 (March, 1975), pp. 180-186.

Bechtel, Leland P. "The Detection and Remediation of Learning Disabilities." Androscoggin County Task Force on Social Welfare, Inc., Lewiston, Maine, 1975.

Becker, Laurence, D. "Conceptual Tempo and the Early Detection of Learning Problems." Journal of Learning Disabilities. Vol. 9, No. 7 (August/September 1976), pp. 433-442.

Bell, Anne E., et al. "Reading Retardation: A 12-year Prospective Study." *Journal of Pediatrics*. Vol. 91, No. 3 (September 1977), pp. 363-370.

Bell, Joan P. "Identification of kindergarten children with learning difficulties." Saskatchewan School Trustees Association, Regina, Saskatchewan (Research Centre Report #40), 1977.

Bell, V.H. "Educator's approach to assessing preschool visually handicapped children." *Education of the Visually Handicapped*. Vol. 7 (October, 1975), pp. 84-89.

Benton, Arthur. "Developmental Dyslexia." *Journal of Pediatric Psychology*. Vol. 1, No. 3 (1976), pp. 28-31.

Bisiar, M.R. "Have a Humpty Dumpty week; readiness skills test." *Instructor*. Vol. 85 (April 1976), p. 95.

Body, P. "Pre-school children at risk." *Early Years*. Vol. 1, No. 2 (1974), pp. 19-20.

Bone, Jan. "Peotone Fights School Failure." *American Education*. Vol. 13, No. 1 (January/February 1977), pp. 32-35.

Boothman, Rosemary, et al. "Predictive Value of Early Developmental Examination." *Archives of Disease in Childhood*. Vol. 51, No. 6 (June 1976), pp. 430-434.

Bradley, E. "Screen them early! Potential learning problems in the kindergarten child." *Academic Therapy*. Vol. 10, (Spring 1975), pp. 305-308.

"Breaking the Cycle of Failure: Diagnostic and Prescriptive Services for Children and Adolescents." *Focus* (The Psychiatric Institute). Fall 1977, pp. 20-23.

Brenton, Beatrice White, and Gilmore, Doug. "An Operational Definition of Learning Disabilities (Cognitive Domain) Using WISC Full Scale IQ and Peabody Individual Achievement Test Scores." *Psychology in the Schools*. Vol. 13, No. 4 (October 1976), pp. 427-432.

Brown, Don A. "What Are the Issues?" Sight-Saving Review. Vol. 46, No. 2 (Summer 1976), pp. 59-63.

Buktenica, N.A. "Identification of potential learning disorders." Journal of Learning Disabilities. Vol. 4 (August 1971), pp. 379-383.

Bunner, Richard T. "Ohio's Comprehensive Vision Project." Sight-Saving Review. Vol. 43, No. 2 (Summer 1973).

Bush, Wilma Jo, and Waugh, Kenneth W. Diagnosing Learning Disabilities. (2nd ed.) Columbus, Ohio: Charles E. Merrill Publishing Co., 1976.

Buttram, J., et al. "Prediction of school readiness and early grade achievement by classroom teachers; Hayes early identification listening response test." Educational Psychological Measurement. Vol. 36, (Summer 1976), pp. 543-546.

Cartwright, Carol A., and Cartwright, G. Phillip. "Competencies for Prevention of Learning Problems in Early Childhood Education." Educational Horizons. Vol. 53, No. 4 (Summer 1975), pp. 151-157.

Casey, Jean M. "Station to Station Screening." Early Years. Vol. 7, No. 8 (April 1977), pp. 41, 50.

Cashman, William E. (ed.), et al. "Position Paper on Learning Disabilities." Northeast Area Learning Resource Center, Hightstown, N.J., 1976.

Chaikin, Rosalind B., et al. "Visual Performance Manual." Nassau County Board of Cooperative Educational Services, Jericho, N.Y. 1976.

Chalfant, J.C., and Foster, G.E. "Identifying learning disabilities in the classroom." Slow Learning Child. Vol. 21, No. 1 (March 1974), pp. 3-14.

Chalfant, James C., and King, Frank S. "An Approach to Operationalizing the Definition of Learning Disabilities." Journal of Learning Disabilities. Vol. 9, No. 4 (April 1976), pp. 228-243.

Chapman, Darral G., and Nolde, Susanne V.L. "Early Identification of Learning Problems." (Chapman) "Relationship Between Sensori-Motor development and the Underachiever." (Nolde). Audio cassette of a presentation at the Reaching Children conferences on hyperactivity and learning disabilities. New York Institute for Child Development, 1976.

"Children's Centre Program in Yarmouth...Most Advanced in Canada." Rehabilitation Digest. Vol. 7, No. 3 (Spring 1976), pp. 4-5.

Clements, Anna. "Expert Tells How to Cope with Learning Disabilities." Un Nuevo Dia. Vol. 2, No. 1 (Spring 1976).

Clements, J.E., et al. "Programming evaluation procedure: A diagnostic and evaluation instrument for classroom teachers." Educational Technology. Vol. 15 (March 1975), pp. 50-54.

Clements, S.D. "Early identification, the multi-disciplinary diagnosis, and the educational management of children with learning disabilities." A lecture for teachers and a discussion with university staff. Melbourne, Specific Learning Difficulties Association of Victoria (1970?).

Cohen, Marilyn Aronin. Teacher Judgment Concerning Arithmetic Disabilities as Accounted for by a Functional Assessment Battery. University of Washington, 1975.

Cole, Sherwood O., and Moore, Samuel F. "The Hyperkinetic Child Syndrome: The Need for Reassessment." Child Psychiatry and Human Development. Vol. 7, No. 2 (Winter 1976).

Coleman, Laurence J. "An Impending Crisis: The Disappearance of Exceptionalities." Education and Training of the Mentally Retarded. Vol. 12, No. 2 (April 1977), pp. 151-153.

Coleman, J. Michael, and Davis, Earl E. "Learning Disabilities: Ten Years Later." Peabody Journal of Education. Vol. 53, No. 3 (April 1976), pp. 180-186.

Colligan, Robert C. "Concurrent Validity of the Myklebust Pupil Rating Scale in a Kindergarten Population." *Journal of Learning Disabilities.* Vol. 10, No. 5 (May 1977), pp. 317-320.

Conference on Identifying and Helping Overcome Specific Learning Problems, Batchelor Education Village, Darwin, 1973. Darwin Department of Education, Northern Territory Branch, 1973.

Conference on Identifying and Helping Overcome Specific Learning Problems, Batchelor Education Village, May 27-June 1, 1974. Darwin Department of Education, Northern Territory Branch, 1974. 1 vol. (various pagings).

Cowgill, M.L. "Predicting learning disabilities from kindergarten reports." *Journal of Learning Disabilities.* Vol. 6 (November 1973), pp. 577-582.

Critchley, MacDonald, Lerner, Janet W., and McLeod, John. "Reading and Dyslexia," in *Learning Disabilities: Selected ACLD papers.* Edited by Samuel A. Kirk and Jeanne McRae McCarthy. Boston: Houghton Mifflin Company, 1975.

Currie, Winifred. "Proposing a Model Assessment and Intervention Program for Learning Disabled Adolescents in a Typical School Population." Paper presented at the International Federation of Learning Disabilities. (Second international scientific conference, Brussels, Belgium, January 3-7, 1975.)

Danhauer, Jeffrey L., and Singh, Sadanand. "A Cross Language Study of Speech Production of Children in Audio and Audio-Visual Modalities." *Acta Symbolica.* Vol. 4, No. 2 (Fall 1973), pp. 29-45.

Davis, William E. "A Comparison of Teacher Referral and Pupil Self-Referral Measures Relative to Perceived School Adjustment." Paper presented at the Annual International Convention, the Council for Exceptional Children. Chicago, Illinois, April 4-9, 1976.

Denhoff, Eric. "Learning Disabilities: An Office Approach." *Pediatrics.* Vol. 58, No. 3 (September 1976).

De Quiros, Julio B. "Diagnosis of Vestibular Disorders in the Learning Disabled." *Journal of Learning Disabilities*. Vol. 9, No. 1 (January 1976), pp. 39-47.

DeRuiter, J.A., et al. "Learning disability classification by Bayesian aggregation of test results." *Journal of Learning Disabilities*. Vol. 8 (June 1975), pp. 365-372.

DeWitt, Frances B. "Tear Off the Label: The Older Student and SLD." *Academic Therapy*. Vol. 13, No. 1 (September 1977).

Dickman, Irving R. "What Can We Do About Limited Vision?" Public Affairs Committee, Inc. New York, 1973.

Divoky, Diane. "Is This Screening Test Worth $1,319,638.50?" *Learning*. Vol. 5, No. 9 (May/June 1977), pp. 66-72.

Dlugokinski, E., et al. "Preschoolers at risk; social, emotional and cognitive considerations." *Psychology in the Schools*. Vol. 13 (April 1976), pp. 134-139.

Doehring, Donald G., and Swisher, Linda P. "Tone Decay and Hearing Threshold Level in Sensorineural Loss." *Journal of Speech and Hearing Research*. Vol. 14, No. 2 (June 1971), pp. 345-349.

Donah, Carol Elizabeth Hamm. "Concurrent, Predictive, and Construct Validation of the Slingerland Screening Tests for Identifying Children with Specific Language Disability." Kent State University, 1976.

Dusewicz, R.A. "Cognitively orientated prekindergarten for children at developmental risk." *Reading Improvement*. Vol. 11 (Winter, 1974), pp. 31-38.

Early, G.H., et al. "Classroom evaluation of learning disabilities; Screening tests for identifying children with specific language disability." *Educational Technology*. Vol. 11 (September 1971), pp. 40-43.

Early Prevention of School Failure: Illinois Title III ESEA Project. Bureau of Elementary and Secondary Education. Springfield: Illinois State Office of the Superintendent of Public Instruction, 1974.

"Early screening programs; Early and Periodic screening, diagnosis, and treatment; realities, risks, and possibilities; symposium." *American Journal of Orthopsychology*. Vol. 48 (January 1978), pp. 4-139.

Eaves, L.C., et al. "Early Identification of Learning Disabilities; A follow-up study." *Journal of Learning Disabilities*. Vol. 7 (1974), pp. 632-638.

Edwards, E. "Emerging needs of children; learning problems in preschool children." *Australian Preschool Quarterly*. Vol. 11, No. 3 (February 1971), pp. 10-16.

Elkind, Joel. "The Gifted Child with Learning Disabilities." *School Psychology Digest*. Vol. 5, No. 3 (Summer 1976), pp. 56-58.

Elkins, J. (ed.). "The identification and treatment of children with learning disabilities." Papers of 4th Annual Seminar in Special Education. St. Lucia, University of Queensland, Fred and Eleanor Schonell Educational Research Centre, 1973.

Ensminger, E. Eugene (ed.). *A Handbook on Secondary Programs for the Learning Disabled Adolescent: Some Guidelines*. Georgia State University, Atlanta, Department of Special Education, 1976.

Evans, Joyce S. *A Project to Develop Curriculum for Four-Year-Old Handicapped Mexican American Children*. Vol. 2 of 2 volumes. Southwest Educational Development Lab., Austin, Texas, November 1974.

Evans, Joyce S. *A Project to Develop Curriculum for Four-Year-Old Handicapped Mexican American Children*. Vol. 1 of 2 volumes. Southwest Educational Development Lab., Austin, Texas, November 1974.

Evans, Joyce. *Identification and Supplementary Instruction for Handicapped Children in a Regular Bilingual Program*. Southwest Educational Development Laboratory, Austin, Texas, 1976.

Evans, Roy. "The prediction of educational handicaps: a longitudinal study." *Educational Research*. Vol. 19 (November 1976), pp. 57-68.

Fairbanks, Dwight W. *Helping Eliminate Early Learning Disabilities (HEELD): An Adopter's Guide*. Central School District 6, Oregon. 1976.

Fankhauser, Glenda, et al. *Circle Preschool: The First Chance Project. Classroom Screening. A Title VI-C Project*. (Piedmont, Ca.: Alpha Plus Corp., 1977).

Federici, Louise, et al. "Use of the Meeting Street School Screening Test and the Myklebust Pupil Rating Scale with First-Grade Black Urban Children." *Psychology in the Schools*. Vol. 13, No. 4 (October 1976), pp. 386-389.

Ferinden, W.E., jr., and Jacobson, S. "Early identification of learning disabilities." *Journal of Learning Disabilities*. Vol. 3 (November 1970), pp. 589-593.

Findlay, Robert C. "Auditory Dysfunction Accompanying Noise-Induced Hearing Loss." *Journal of Speech and Hearing Disorders*. Vol. 41, No. 3 (August 1976).

Fisher, Lee I. "Efficiency and Effectiveness of Using a Portable Audiometric Booth in School Hearing Conservation Programs." *Language, Speech, and Hearing Services in Schools*. Vol. 7, No. 4 (October 1976), pp. 242-249.

Flood, B. "Better early than never." *Education of the Visually Handicapped*. Vol. 9 (Summer 1977), pp. 36-40.

Flook, W.M., and Velicer, W.F. "School readiness and teacher's ratings: a validation study; Preschool screening system." *Psychology in the Schools*. Vol. 14 (April 1977), pp. 140-146.

Flynn, T.M. "Behavioural components of school readiness; preschool migrant child." *Journal of Experimental Education*. Vol. 44 (Fall 1975), pp. 40-45.

Flynn, T.M., and Flynn, L.A. "Evaluation of the predictive ability of five screening measures administered during kindergarten." *Journal of Experimental Education*. Vol. 46 (Spring 1978), pp. 65-70.

Forness, S.R., and Esveldt, K.C. "Prediction of high-risk kindergarten children through classroom observation." Journal of Special Education. Vol. 9 (Winter 1975), pp. 375-387.

Forness, S.R., et al. "Cluster of observable behaviour in high-risk kindergarten children." Psychology in the Schools. Vol. 12 (July 1975), pp. 263-269.

Forness, Steven, et al. "Follow-Up of High Risk Children Identified in Kindergarten Through Direct Classroom Observation." Psychology in the Schools. Vol. 13, No. 1 (January 1976), pp. 45-49.

Forness, S.R., et al. "Eventual school placement of kindergarteners observed as high risk in the classroom." Psychology in the Schools. Vol. 14 (July 1977), pp. 315-317.

Frankenburg, William K., and Camp, Bonnie, W. (eds.). Pediatric Screening Tests. Springfield: Charles C. Thomas, 1975.

Frankenburg, William K., et al. "Implications of Early Screening for Later Development." Final Report, July 1, 1974 - February 26, 1976. Colorado University, Denver, Medical Center.

Frostig, Marrianne, Rosser, Pearl L., and Bartlett, Charles H. "Screening, Diagnosis and Assessment." in Learning Disabilities: Selected ACLD Papers. Edited by Samuel A. Kirk and Jeanne McRae McCarthy. Boston: Houghton Mifflin Company, 1975.

Fuller, G.B., and Friedrich, D. "Three diagnostic patterns of reading disabilities." Academic Therapy. Vol. 10 (Winter 1974/75) pp. 219-231.

Fulmer, K.A., and Metcalfe, B. "Early identification of learning problems using Purdue perceptual-motor survey and teacher's ratings." Graylands Education News. Vol. 8 (June 1973), pp. 26-29.

Gallagher, J.J., and Bradley, R.H. "Early identification of developmental difficulties." National Society for the Study of Education Yearbook. 71 pt. Vol. 2 (1972), pp. 87-122.

Gardner, Harvey J. "Application of a High-Frequency Consonant Discrimination Word List in Hearing-Aid Evaluation." *Journal of Speech and Hearing Disorders*. Vol. 36 (August 1971), pp. 354-355.

Gearhart, Bill R., and Weishahn, Mel W. *The Handicapped Child in the Regular Classroom*. St. Louis, Mo.: C.V. Mosby Co., 1976.

Gerard, Joyce. *Correcting Handwriting Problems*. Teacher guide and videocassette. Agency for Instructional Television, 1974.

Gerwin, Kenneth S., and Glorig, Aram (eds.). *Detection of Hearing Loss and Ear Disease in Children*. Springfield, Ill.: Charles C. Thomas, 1974.

Giolas, Thomas G., and Randolph, Kenneth. *Basic Audiometry Including Impedance Measurement*. Lincoln, Neb.: Cliff Notes, 1977

Gitter, L.L. "Story of Mopsy; a diagnostic tool; informal teaching-testing using the drawings of children." *Journal for Special Educators of the Mentally Retarded*. Vol. 12 (Fall 1975), pp. 42-49.

Givens, Gregg D., and Seidemann, Michael F. "Middle Ear Measurements in a Difficult to Test Mentally Retarded Population." *Mental Retardation*. Vol. 15 (October 1977), pp. 40-42.

Goleman, Daniel. "Breakthrough in Diagnosis: A New Computer Test of the Brain." *Psychology Today*. Vol. 9 (May 1976), pp. 44-48.

Goodman, Libby, and Mann, Lester. *Learning Disabilities in the Secondary School: Issues and Practices*. New York: Grune and Stratton, subsidiary of Harcourt Brace Jovanovich, 1976.

Gouge, Betty Merle Gage. *A Reliability and Validity Study of the VADS Test for Screening Learning Disabilities of Second Graders with Teachers as Examiners*. Texas Woman's University, 1975.

Gould, Roberta Berkley. *Kindergarten Screening: An Evaluation of the Use of Psychoneurological Testing in Predicting Learning Problems*. Fordham University, 1977.

Graf, Mercedes. "A School Psychologist's Perceptions of Learning Disabilities in Three-Year-Old Children in an Early Childhood Center." Paper presented at the Illinois Council for Exceptional Children, Chicago, October 1975.

Grassi, Fay Ruth. *Predicting Special Class Placement of Elementary School Pupils with the Use of the Burks' Behavior Rating Scale*. University of Northern Colorado, 1976.

Gresson, A.D., and Carter, D.G., sr. "In search of the potentially gifted: suggestions for the school administrator." *Clearing House*. Vol. 50 (April 1977), pp. 369-371.

Grill, J. Jeffrey. "Identification of Learning-Disabled Adolescents." *Academic Therapy*. Vol. 13, No. 1 (September 1977), pp. 23-28.

Gunderson, B.V. "Diagnosis of learning disabilities; the team approach." *Journal of Learning Disabilities*. Vol. 4 (February 1971), pp. 107-113.

Hagin, R.A., et al. "Clinical-diagnostic use of the WPPSI in predicting learning disabilities in grade 1." *Journal of Special Education*. Vol. 5 (Fall 1971), pp. 221-232.

Hakim, C.S. "Task analysis: one alternative; diagnosis of a mild learning disability." *Academic Therapy*. Vol. 10 (Winter 1974/75), pp. 201-209.

Hallahan, Daniel P., and Kauffman, James M. *Introduction to Learning Disabilities: A Psycho-Behavioral Approach*. Englewood Cliffs, N.J.: Prentice Hall, Inc., 1976.

Hammer, Max. "A Teacher's Guide to the Detection of Emotional Disturbance in the Elementary School Child." *Journal of Learning Disabilities*. Vol. 3, No. 10 (October 1970), pp. 517-519.

Hammill, Donald D. "Defining 'LD' for Programmatic Purposes." *Academic Therapy*. Vol. 12, No. 1 (Fall 1976), pp. 29-37.

Harley, Randall K., and Lawrence, G. Allen. *Visual Impairment in the Schools*. Springfield, Ill.: Charles C. Thomas, 1977.

Hawthorne, L.W., and Larsen, S.C. "Predictive validity and reliability of the basic school skills inventory." *Journal of Learning Disabilities*. Vol. 10 (January 1977), pp. 44-50.

Hayes, M., et al. "Validity and reliability of a simple device for readiness screening; the Hayes early identification listening response test." *Educational and Psychological Measurement*. Vol. 35 (Summer 1975), pp. 495-498.

Helms, David Marvin. *The Familial Association of Specific Learning Disabilities*. California School of Professional Psychology, 1976.

Helvey, T.C. "Learning disability measurement with the synchroencephalograph." *Journal of Experimental Education*. Vol. 44 (Fall 1975), pp. 18-25.

Hess, R.J., and Hahn, R.T., 2nd. "Prediction of school failure and the Hess school readiness scale." *Psychology in the Schools*. Vol. 11 (April 1974), pp. 134-136.

Hession, Lucy Anne. "Training Special and Regular Educators in the Observation, Identification and Management of Children (k-3) with Learning Handicaps." Final Report. Maryland State Department of Education, Baltimore. Division of Instruction. 1974.

Hiltbrunner, C.L., and Vasa, S.F. "Watch the children; precision referring of learning disabled." *Academic Therapy*. Vol. 10 (Winter 1974/75), pp. 167-172.

Hinton, G.G., and Knights, R.M. "Children with learning problems: academic history, academic prediction, and adjustment three years after assessment." *Exceptional Children*. Vol. 37 (March 1971), pp. 513-519.

Hobbs, N., et al. "Classifying children; summary of the final report of the project on classification of exceptional children." Children Today. Vol. 4 (July 1975), pp. 21-25.

Hogan, Gwendolyn R., and Ryan, Nell J. "Evaluation of the Child with a Learning Disorder." Pediatrics. Vol. 58, No. 3 (September 1976), pp. 407-409.

Hokanson, Dean T., and Jospe, Michael. The Search for Cognitive Giftedness in Exceptional Children. 1976.

Hollinshead, Merrill T. "Pre-School Program for Emotionally Disturbed, Language and Perceptually Impaired Children (Title VI) Evaluation Period (December 1974 - June 1975). Evaluation Report." New York City Board of Education, Brooklyn, N.Y., Office of Educational Evaluation. 1975.

Holmes, D.J. "Disturbances of the preschool and very young school child; learning disabilities." Journal of School Health. Vol. 45 (April 1975), pp. 210-216.

"How to find the children in your schools who most need special education." American School Board Journal. Vol. 163 (November 1976), pp. 44-45.

Hull, Raymond H. "Group vs. Individual Screening in Public School Audiometry." Colorado Journal of Educational Research. Vol. 13, No. 1 (1973), pp. 6-9.

Humes, C.E. "Early learning disabilities identification: a report." Academic Therapy. Vol. 10 (Summer 1975), pp. 419-425.

Hutson, B.A. "Psychological testing: misdiagnosis and half-diagnosis." Psychological Scholar. Vol. 11 (October 1974), pp. 388-391.

"Infant Appraisal." (film). National Audiovisual Center, Washington, 1976.

Jackson, R.M., et al. "Methods and results of an every-child program for the early identification of developmental deficits." Psychology in the Schools. Vol. 10 (October 1973), pp. 421-426.

Jacobs, Jacqueline E., and Sacatsh, Jean. "Kindergarten Diagnostic Assessment of Learning Style." Paper presented at the International Scientific Federation of Learning Disabilities (Second International Scientific Conference, Brussels, Belgium, January 3-7, 1975.)

Jaffe, Burton F. (ed.). Hearing Loss in Children: A Comprehensive Treatise. Baltimore, MD: University Park Press, 1977.

Jaffe, D.K. "Ready, set, go! New Hampshire school readiness project." American Education. Vol. 6 (August 1970), pp. 9-12.

Jamieson, Monika, et al. Towards Integration: A Study of Blind and Partially Sighted Children in Ordinary Schools. Atlantic Highland, N.J.: Humanities Press, Inc., 1977.

Jenkins, J.R., and Pony, D. "Standardized achievement tests: how useful for special education?" Exceptional Children. Vol. 44 (March 1978), pp. 448-453.

Johnson, Doris J., et al., in Learning Disabilities: Selected ACLD papers. Edited by Samuel A. Kirk and Jeanne McRae McCarthy. Boston: Houghton Mifflin Company, 1975.

Johnson, E.W. "Let's Look at the Child Not the Audiogram." Volta Review, Volume 69. Washington: Alexander Graham Bell Association for Deaf, 1967.

Johnson, V.M. "Salient features and sorting factors in diagnosis and classification of exceptional children." Peabody Journal of Education. Vol. 52 (January 1975), pp. 142-149.

Jones, R. Wayne. The Target Groups: Description of Learning Disabled and Normal Subjects Participating in Prototype Evaluation Studies. Georgia State University, Atlanta, 1975.

Kane, J., and Gill, R.P. "Implications of the Purdue pegboard as a screening device." Journal of Learning Disabilities. Vol. 5 (January 1972), pp. 32-36.

Kappelman, M.M. "Learning disabilities: a team approach to diagnosis and prescription." *Educational Leadership*. Vol. 32 (May 1975), pp. 513-516.

Karnes, M.B., and Bertschi, J.D. "Identifying and educating gifted/talented non-handicapped and handicapped preschoolers." *Teaching Exceptional Children*. Vol. 10 (Summer 1978), pp. 114-119.

Kealy, Jean, and McLeod, John. "Learning Disability and Socioeconomic Status." *Journal of Learning Disabilities*. Vol. 9, No. 9 (November 1976), pp. 596-599.

Keiter, Joel L. "Educational Process Evaluation by Teachers." Individual practicum. Nova University, Fort Lauderdale, Fla., 1976.

Kelly, G.R. "Group perceptual screening at first grade level." *Journal of Learning Disabilities*. Vol. 3 (December 1970), pp. 640-644.

Kenney, E.T. "Learning disability: what it is and is not." *Educational Leadership*. Vol. 32 (May 1975), pp. 507-510.

Keogh, B.K. (ed.). "Early identification of children with potential learning problems; symposium." *Journal of Special Education*. Vol. 4 (Summer 1970), pp. 306-363.

Keogh, Barbara K. "Early ID: Selective Perception or Perceptive Selection?" *Academic Therapy*. Vol. 12, (Spring 1977), pp. 267-274.

Keogh, B.K., and Becker, L.D. "Early detection of learning problems; questions, cautions, and guidelines." *Exceptional Children*. Vol. 40 (September 1973), pp. 5-11.

Kephart, W.B. "Prekindergarten screening clinics." *Phi Delta Kappan*. Volume 55 (March 1974), p. 459. Reply: Orlando, C.P. and Grund, W.E. *Phi Delta Kappan*. Vol. 56 (October 1974), p. 148.

Kershaw, John. *People with Dyslexia: Report of a Working Party Commissioned by the British Council for Rehabilitation of the Disabled.* British Council for Rehabilitation of the Disabled, London. 1974.

Kessler, Henry H. *Disability: Determination and Evaluation.* Philadelphia, Penn.: Lea and Febiger, 1970.

Kinsbourne, M. "Diagnosis and treatment of school problems." *Australian Journal of Remedial Education.* Volume 7, No. 2 (1975), pp. 7-14.

Kirk, S.A., and Elkins, J. "Identifying developmental discrepancies at the preschool level." *Journal of Learning Disabilities.* Vol. 8 (August 1975), pp. 417-419.

Kirk, Samuel A. and McCarthy, Jeanne (eds.). *Learning Disabilities: Selected ACLD Papers.* Boston: Houghton Mifflin Company, 1975.

Kirschenbaum, Daniel S., et al. "The Effectiveness of a Mass Screening Procedure in an Early Intervention Program." *Psychology in the Schools.* Vol. 14, No. 4 (October 1977), pp. 400-406.

Klein, A.E. "Validity of the Screening test of academic readiness in predicting achievement in first and second grades." *Educational and Psychological Measurement.* Vol. 37 (Summer 1977), pp. 493-499.

Kleisinger, G.J. "Individual readiness and diagnostic test for pre-school evaluation and early intervention; Regina rural health region. Saskatchewan, Canada." *Journal of School Health.* Vol. 43, (April 1973), pp. 233-235.

Koppitz, Elizabeth Munsterberg. "Strategies for Diagnosis and Identification of Children with Behavior and Learning Problems." *Behavioral Disorders.* Vol. 2, No. 3 (May 1977), pp. 136-140.

Kratoville, Betty Lou. "Dealing with Public Schools." *Academic Therapy.* Vol. 13, No. 2 (November 1977), pp. 225-232.

Kuhlberg, J.M., and Gershman, E.S. "School readiness: studies of assessment procedures and comparison of three types of programming for immature 5-yr.-olds." Psychology in the Schools. Vol. 10 (October 1973), pp. 410-420.

Kurtz, P.D., et al. "Issues concerning the early identification of handicapped children." Journal of School Psychology. Vol. 15 (Summer 1977), pp. 136-140.

Kurtz, R., and Spiker, J. "Slow or Learning disabled; is there a difference?" The Arithmetic Teacher. Vol. 23 (December 1976), pp. 617-622.

Lall, Geeta Rani. Team Approach in Assessment and Treatment of Children with Learning Disabilities. Andrews University, Department of Education, Berrian Springs, Michigan. 1976.

Lanier, Joe Harrison. Cognitive Abilities Test Score Patterns for Possible Utilization in Identifying Children with Learning Disabilities. Duke University, 1976.

Larsen, Stephen C., et al. "The Use of Selected Perceptual Tests in Differentiating Between Normal and Learning Disabled Children." Journal of Learning Disabilities. Vol. 9, No. 2 (February, 1976), pp. 85-90. "Discussion." Journal of Learning Disabilities. Vol. 9 (November 1976), pp. 322-327, 455-456, 609.

Larson, Vicki. "A Comparison of Screening Models Under Chapter 115." Bureau Memorandum. Vol. 18, No. 1 (Fall 1976), pp. 2-4.

Leaky, M.S. "Let's be culture-fair; non-verbal individual readiness test." American Education. Vol. 6 (October 1970), p. 34.

"Learning Disabilities--Identification and Assessment: 1977 Topical Bibliography." Council for Exceptional Children. Reston, Va., 1977.

"Learning disability; role of the school: symposium." Educational Leadership. Vol. 32 (May 1975), pp. 499-519.

Leong, C.K. "Detection of Children with Learning Problems: Some Considerations." *Mental Retardation Bulletin*. Vol. 5, No. 1 (Spring 1977).

Lesiak, W.J., jr. "Screening primary-grade children for educational handicaps: a teacher-administered battery." *Psychology in the Schools*. Vol. 10 (January 1973), pp. 88-101.

Lesiak, W.J., jr., and Wait, J.A. "Diagnostic kindergarten: initial step in the identification and programming of children with learning problems." *Psychological Scholar*. Vol. 11 (July 1974), pp. 282-290.

Lessler, K., and Bridges, J.S. "Prediction of learning problems in a rural setting: can we improve on readiness tests?" *Journal of Learning Disabilities*. Vol. 6 (Fall 1973), pp. 90-94.

Leton, D.A. "Structure of the Stanford diagnostic reading test in relation to the assessment of learning-disabled pupils. *Psychology in the Schools*. Vol. 11 (January 1974), pp. 40-47.

Levin, Susan, and Erber, Norman P. "A Vision Screening Program for Deaf Children." *Volta Review*. Vol. 78, No. 2 (February/March 1976), pp. 90-99.

Levenson, D. "Where do they belong? Placing children by developmental level." *Teacher*. Vol. 94 (March 1977), pp. 54-56.

Lin-Fu, Jane S. *Vision Screening of Children*. Public Health Service, Washington, D.C. 1971.

Logan, B.A. "Kindergarten screening program for learning disabilities." *Journal of School Health*. Vol. 45 (September 1975), pp. 413-414.

Loss, Barbara Lynn. *The Identification of Aptitude Describers Common to High-Risk Preschool Children with Potential Learning Problems*. Wayne State University, 1976.

Love, Harold D. *Exceptional Children in a Modern Society*. Dubuque, Iowa: Wm. C. Brown Book Company.

Magliocca, L.A., et al. "Early identification of handicapped children through a frequency sampling technique." *Exceptional Children*. Vol. 43 (April 1977), pp. 414-420.

Maitland, S., et al. "Early school screening practices." *Journal of Learning Disabilities*. Vol. 7 (December 1974), pp. 645-649.

Malone, C.E., and Moonan, W.J. "Behavioural identification of gifted children." *Gifted Children Quarterly*. Vol. 19 (Winter, 1975), pp. 301-306.

Mardell, C., and Goldenberg, G. "For prekindergarten screening information: DIAL (Developmental indicators for the assessment of learning)." *Journal of Learning Disabilities*. Vol. 8 (March 1975), pp. 140-147.

Mardell, Carol, and Goldenberg, Dorothea S. "The Predictive Validation of a Pre-Kindergarten Screening Test." Paper presented at the International Scientific Conference of IFLD. Montreal, August 1976.

Margolis, Howard. "The Kindergarten Auditory Screening Test as a Predictor of Reading Disability." *Psychology in the Schools.* Vol. 13, No. 4 (October 1976), pp. 399-403.

Marks, M.B. "Recognition of the allergic child at school: visual and auditory signs." *Journal of School Health*. Vol. 44 (May 1974), pp. 277-284.

Maurer, Stephan Richard. *First Impressions of Normal and Emotionally Disturbed Children*. Illinois Institute of Technology, 1975.

Mauser, August J. *Assessing the Learning Disabled: Selected Instruments*. San Rafael, Ca.: Academic Therapy Publications, 1976.

Mavrogenes, Nancy A., et al. "A Guide to Tests of Factors That Inhibit Learning to Read." *Reading Teacher*. Vol. 29, No. 4 (January 1976).

McCarthy, Jeanne McRae. *A Public School Program of Remediation for Children with Specific Learning Disabilities. Final Report.* Schaumburg (Illinois) Community Consolidated School District 54, October 1973.

McElgunn, Barbara. "Learning Disability: The Need for Medical Research." *Journal of Learning Disabilities.* Vol. 9, No. 6 (June/July, 1976).

McGrady, Harold J., and Anderson, Carolyn S. *Screening and Identification Procedures in the Child Service Demonstration Programs.* University of Arizona, Tucson, Department of Special Education, June 1974.

Mecham, M.J., et al. "Use of the Utah test of language development for screening language disabilities." *Journal of Learning Disabilities.* Vol. 6 (October 1973), pp. 524-527.

Meier, John H. *Developmental and Learning Disabilities: Evaluation Management, and Prevention in Children.* Baltimore, Md.: University Park Press, 1976.

Mercer, Cecil D., and Trifiletti, John H. "The Development of Screening Procedures for the Early Detection of Children with Learning Problems." *Journal of School Health.* Vol. 47, No. 9 (November 1977).

Merenda, Peter F., et al. "Identification Scale." *Psychology in the Schools.* Vol. 14, No. 3 (July 1977).

Mills, J.C. "That all children may learn: all-volunteer preschool screening program, Pleasant Valley, N.Y." *Teacher.* Vol. 90 (December 1972), pp. 36-40.

Monteith, Mary K. "ERIC/RCS Report: Screening and Assessment Programs for Young Children: Reading Readiness and Learning Problems." *Language Arts.* Vol. 53, No. 8 (November/December 1976), pp. 920-924.

Mullen, J. "Identifying LD kindergarten children." *Academic Therapy.* Vol. 11 (Fall 1975), pp. 117-118.

Munns, Evangeline Francis. *The Development of a Teachers' Observation Scale for the Identification of Children with Learning Disabilities.* York University, 1971.

Nazzaro, J. "Head start for the handicapped: what's been accomplished?" Exceptional Child. Vol. 41 (October, 1974), pp. 103-106.

Neel, Richard S. "A Psychometric Investigation of Identification of Children with Academic Difficulties." Journal of Special Education. Vol. 10, No. 1 (Spring 1976), pp. 91-95.

Nichol, H. "Children with learning disabilities referred to psychiatrists: a follow-up study." Journal of Learning Disabilities. Vol. 7 (Fall 1974), pp. 118-122.

Novack, H.S., et al. "Scale for early detection of children with learning problems." Exceptional Children. Vol. 40 (October 1973), pp. 98-105.

Nurss, J.R. "Testing for readiness." Early Years. Vol. 8 (February 1978), pp. 62-63.

O'Connor, Katherine H. Removing Roadblocks in Reading: A Guidebook for Teaching Perceptually Handicapped Children. St. Petersburg, Fl.: Johnny Reads, Inc. 1976

Ohlson, E. Lamonte. Identification of Specific Learning Disabilities. Champaign, Ill.: Research Press, 1978.

Otey, J.W. "Identification of Gifted Students." Psychology in the Schools. Vol. 15 (January 1978), pp. 16-21.

Ozer, M.N., et al. "Assessment of children with learning problems: an in-service teacher training program." Journal of Learning Disabilities. Vol. 7 (November 1974), pp. 539-544.

Ozer, M.N., and Richardson, H.B., jr. "Diagnostic evaluation of children with learning problems: a communication process." Childhood Education. Vol. 48 (Fall 1972), pp. 244-247.

Ozer, M.N., and Richardson, H.B., jr. "Diagnostic evaluation of children with learning problems: a process approach." Journal of Learning Disabilities. Vol. 7 (Fall 1974), pp. 88-92.

Peabody, George. *The PASS Model Project: Administrative Handbook.* College for Teachers, Nashville, Tenn., 1976.

Patton, Carl Vernon. "Selecting Special Students: Who Decides?" *Teachers College Record.* Vol. 78, No. 1 (September 1976), pp. 101-124.

Pines, Maya. "Head Head Start. Bringing up Babies in Brookline." *Education Digest.* Vol. 41, No. 1.

Pope, L., and Haklay, A. "Follow-up study of psychoeducational evaluations sent to schools." *Journal of Learning Disabilities.* Vol. 7 (April 1974), pp. 239-244.

Primary Language Activities. Florida Learning Resources System/Crown. Jacksonville, Fla., 1975.

Proceedings of International Conference on Oral Education of the Deaf. Vol. 1. Clarke School for the Deaf, Northampton, Mass., 1967.

Proger, B.B. "Pupil rating scale: screening for learning disabilities; review." *Journal of Special Education.* Vol. 7 (Fall 1973), pp. 311-317.

Project OPEN 1974-1975 Child Service Demonstration Center Title VI - GC ESEA. Final Report. Brockton Public Schools, Mass., 1975.

Project STRETCH: Mathematics and the Special Student. Module 20 of Strategies for Training Regular Educators to Teach Children with Handicaps. 3/4 inch videotape cassette. Metropolitan Cooperative Educational Service Agency, Atlanta, Ga., 1976.

Ranck, Shirley Ann. *A Factor Analysis of Five Perceptual Motor Tests of First Grade Children.* Fordham University, 1976.

Raskin, L.M., et al. "Teacher as observer for assessment: a guideline." *Young Children.* Vol. 30 (July 1975), pp. 339-344.

Raskin, L.M., and Taylor, W.J. "Problem identification through observation." *Academic Therapy.* Vol. 9 (Fall 1973), pp. 85-89.

Reeves, John F., and Perkins, Mark L. "The Pupil Rating Scale: A Second Look." *Journal of Special Education.* Vol. 10, No. 4 (Winter 1976), pp. 437-439.

Reinherz, H., and Griffin, C.L. "Identifying children at risk: A first step to prevention." *Health Education.* Vol. 8 (July/August 1977), pp. 14-16.

Renzulli, J.S., and Smith L.H. "Two approaches to identification of gifted students." *Exceptional Child.* Vol. 43 (May 1977), pp. 512-518.

Richman, N., and Graham, P.J. "Behavioural screening questionnaire for use with three-year-old children; preliminary findings." *Journal of Child Psychology and Psychiatry and Allied Disciplines.* Vol. 12 (June 1971), pp. 5-33.

Ridsdale, A.M. "Recognition of and intervention in the early stages of learning difficulties," in Speld, Victoria. *Reading difficulty and the intelligent under-achiever.* (Melbourne, 1971), pp. 28-36.

Rogers, George W., and Richmond, Bert O. *Results on the Slosson Drawing Coordination Test with Appalachian Sheltered Workshop Clients.* 1975.

Rosen, Karen, and Minisi, Rena. *Region 9 Task Force on Learning Disabilities: Summary of Proceedings.* March 24-25, 1976.

Rosewell, Florence G., and Natchez, Gladys. *Reading Disability: A Human Approach to Learning.* 3rd edition. New York: Basic Book Publishers, 1977.

Rutter, Michael. *Helping Troubled Children.* New York: Plenum Publishing Co., 1975.

Salvia, J. and Clark, J. "Use of deficits to identify the learning disabled." *Exceptional Children.* Vol. 39 (January 1973), pp. 305-308.

Satz, Paul, et al. "Some Predictive Antecedents of Specific Reading Disability: A Three-Year Follow-Up." *Bulletin of the Orton Society.* Vol. 25 (1975), pp. 91-110.

Sbordone, Melinda Welles. *Early Identification of Educationally High Risk and High Potential Children from Kindergarten Through First Grade.* University of California, 1976.

Schaaf, Sally Eleanor. *Selected Characteristics of Mean Dispersion Scores for the Illinois Test of Psycholinguistic Abilities.* Ohio University, 1976.

Schaer, Hildegard F., and Crump, W. Donald. "Teacher Involvement and Early Identification of Children with Learning Disabilities." *Journal of Learning Disabilities.* Vol. 9, No. 2 (February 1976), pp. 91-95.

Schleifer, M.J. "Early diagnosis: we want to know whether Jimmy is ready to start kindergarten." *Exceptional Parent.* Vol. 8 (February 1978), pp. 14-18.

Schmitt, Barton D. "The Minimal Brain Dysfunction Myth." *American Journal of Diseases of Children.* Vol. 129, No. 11 (November 1975), pp. 1313-1318.

Schmidt, C.R., et al. "Predictive Validity of the Test of auditory perception." *Educational and Psychological Measurement.* Vol. 35 (Winter 1975), pp. 1023, 1027.

"School children at risk: some perspectives of concern." Papers presented at a seminar held at Burwood State College, April 15-16, 1977. Burwood, Vic., Australia, Burwood state College, 1977.

"Screening: more important than ever." *Early Years.* Vol. 8 (February 1978), pp. 32-35.

Seda, M.S.A., and Michael, J.J. "Concurrent validity of the Sprigle school screening readiness test for a sample of preschool and kindergarten children." *Educational and Psychological Measurement."* Vol. 31 (Winter 1971), pp. 995-997.

Senf, G.M., et al. "State initiative in learning disabilities: Illinois' Project SCREEN." *Journal of Learning Disabilities.* Vol. 8 (August-December 1975), pp. 541-547, 524-533, 587-596, 613-623.

Shepherd, M.J. "Learning disabled or slow learner?" *Teacher*. (March 1975), pp. 29-31.

Shepherd, Margaret Jo. "Learning Disabled or Slow Learner?" *School Psychology Digest*. Vol. 5, No. 1 (Winter 1976), pp. 32-35.

Shuttleworth, Alan. "Screening Procedures in the Primary School." *Aspects of Education*. No. 20 (July 1975), pp. 24-30.

Silver, Archie, and Hagin, Rosa A. "Fascinating Journey: Paths to the Prediction and Prevention of Reading Disability." *Bulletin of the Orton Society*. Vol. 25, pp. 24-36.

Silver, Archie A., and Hagin, Rosa A. *SEARCH: A Scanning Instrument for the Identification of Potential Learning Disability*. A Component of the Search and Teach Package. New York: Walker Educational Book Corporation, 1976.

Silverman, I., et al. "Relationships among Token test, age and WISC scores for children with learning problems." *Journal of Learning Disabilities*. Vol. 10 (February 1977), pp. 104-107.

Slack, G. "Child Find." *American Education*. Vol. 12 (December 1976), pp. 29-33.

Smith, S.A., and Solanto, J.R. "Approach to preschool evaluations." *Psychology in the Schools.* Vol. 8 (April 1971), pp. 142-147.

Smith, Don A., and Wilborn, Bobbie L. "Specific Predictors of Learning Disabilities." *Academic Therapy*. Vol. 12, No. 4 (Summer 1977), pp. 471-477.

Snyder, C.R. "The Psychological Implications of Being Color Blind." *Journal of Special Education*. Vol. 7, No. 1 (Spring 1973), pp. 51-54.

Sommers, Paul A. *Teaching Children with Learning Problems*. 1976.

Sower, R. and Covert, R. "Identifying preschoolers with special needs; a county-wide project to help plan future special services in the public schools." Education and Training of the Mentally Retarded. Vol. 10 (April 1975), pp. 84-90.

Spalding, Norma Vivian Snyder. The Validation of a Neurological Screening Test for Learning Disabilities. University of California at Berkeley, 1972.

Spalding, Norma V. "Research with QNST: A Review." Paper presented at the International Scientific Conference of IFLD, Montreal, August 9-13, 1976.

Spalding, Norma V., and Geiser, Marilyn Charlesworth. "Teacher Testing with the QNST." Academic Therapy. Vol. 13, No. 3 (January 1978), pp. 313-321.

Spencer, O., et al. "A multidisciplinary approach to assessment (of children with behaviour, learning and communication disorders)." Inside Education. Vol. 69, No. 2 (Autumn 1975), pp. 10-16. (Summary of paper read at Conference of the Association for Children with Learning Disabilities, University of New South Wales.)

Stanley, J.C. "Identifying and nurturing the intellectually gifted." Phi Delta Kappan. Vol. 58 (November 1976), pp. 234-237.

Stephens, M. Irene, and Daniloff, Raymond. "A Methodological Study of Factors Affecting the Judgment of Misarticulated s." Journal of Communications Disorders. Vol. 10, No. 3 (September 1977), pp. 207-220.

Sterling, Harold M., and Sterling, Patricia J. "Experiences with the QNST." Academic Therapy. Vol. 12, No. 3 (Spring 1977), pp. 339-342.

Sterling, Harold M., and Sterling, Patricia J. "Further Experiences with the QNST." Academic Therapy. Vol. 12, No. 4 (Summer 1977), pp. 487-490.

Sullivan, A.R. "Identification of gifted and academically talented black students: a hidden exceptionality." Journal of Special Education. Vol. 7 (Winter 1973), pp. 373-379.

Svobda, James S., and Weidner, William E. "Auditory Verbal Recognition Ability of Aphasic Adults Under Two Conditions of Listening." Acta Symbolica. Vol. 1, No. 1 (Spring 1970), pp. 12-14.

Swanson, M.S., and Jacobson, A. "Evaluation of the S.I.T. for screening children with learning disabilities." Journal of Learning Disabilities. Vol. 3 (June 1970), pp. 318-320.

Sykes, S. "Learning disability in the primary school." Australian Journal of Remedial Education. Vol. 6, No. 2 (June 1974), pp. 19-22.

Taylor, Ian G. The Neurological Mechanisms of Hearing and Speech in Children. Manchester University Press, Washington.

Telegdy, G.A. "Effectiveness of four readiness tests as predictors of first grade academic achievement." Psychology in the Schools. Vol. 12 (January 1975), pp. 4-11.

Telegdy, G.A. "Validity of I.Q. scores derived from readiness screening tests; Screening test of academic readiness." Psychology in the Schools. Vol. 13 (October 1976), pp. 394-396.

Thomas, J.R., and Chissom, B.S. "Prediction of first grade academic performance from kindergarten perceptual motor data." Research Quarterly. Vol. 45 (May 1974), pp. 148-153.

Thompson, M. "Identifying the gifted." National Elementary Principal. Vol. 51 (Fall 1972), pp. 37-44.

Thompson, M. "A Pilot Instrument of Dyslexic-Type Language Difficulties: The Aston Index." Paper presented at the International Federation of Learning Disabilities (Second International Scientific Conference, Brussels, Belgium, January 3 - 7, 1975).

Tobiessen, J., et al. "Relationships between the Schenectady kindergarten rating scales and first grade achievement and adjustment." Psychology in the Schools. Vol. 8 (January 1971), pp. 29-36.

Torrance, E.P. "Non-test indicators of creative talent among disadvantaged children." *Gifted Children Quarterly*. Vol. 17 (Spring 1973), pp. 3-9.

Touwen, Bert C.L., et al. "Neurological Screening of Full-Term Newborn Infants." *Developmental Medicine and Child Neurology*. Vol. 19, No. 6 (December 1977), pp. 739-747.

Ugland, Richard. *Serving Students with Specific Learning Disabilities in Higher Education--A Demonstration Project at Three Minnesota Community Colleges: A Project Evaluation Report*. Rochester Community College, Normandale Community College, Metropolitan Community College, 1976.

Vance, H.B. "Informal assessment techniques with L.D. children." *Academic Therapy*. Vol. 12 (Spring 1977), pp. 291-303.

Vance, Hubert (Booney), et al. "Analysis of Cognitive Abilities for Learning Disabled Children." *Psychology in the Schools*. Vol. 13, No. 4 (October 1976), pp. 477-483.

Van Doorninck, William J., et al. "Infant and Preschool Developmental Screening and Later School Performance." Paper presented at the Society for Pediatric Research, St. Louis, Missouri, April 1976.

Van Noorden, Gunter K. "Chronic Vision Problems of School-Age Children." *Journal of School Health*. Vol. 46, No. 6 (June 1976), pp. 334-337.

VI-G Sec 661, P.L. 91-320. Final Performance Report. October 1976.

Vision and Hearing Screening in Selected Classes for the Mentally Retarded. Michigan Department of Public Health, Detroit Children's Bureau, Welfare Administration, Washington.

Vivian, R.P. *Report on the Early Identification Program of the Board of Education of Windsor, 1974-78*. Toronto: Ministry of Education, Ontario, 1979.

Watkins, Ernest O. *The Watkins Bender-Gestalt Scoring System. Norms, Interpretation and Scoring Manual for Normal Subjects and Subjects with Learning Disabilities*. Academic Therapy Publications, San Rafael, Ca., 1976.

Wedell, K. "Diagnosing learning difficulties: a sequential strategy." *Journal of Learning Disabilities*. Vol. 3 (June 1970), pp. 311-317.

Wedell, K., and Raybould, E.C. (eds.) *The Early Identification of Educationally 'At Risk' Children. Educational Review*. Occasional publications No. 6. Birmingham University, Great Britian, 1976.

Weiner, L. "They spot learning problems early; screening kindergarten children." *Instructor*. Vol. 82 (January 1973), pp. 108-109.

Wendt, R.N. "Kindergarten entrance assessment: is it worth the effort?" *Psychology in the Schools*. Vol. 15 (January 1978), pp. 56-62.

White, M. "Diagnosis of specific learning difficulty." *Education News*. Vol. 14, No. 2 (April 1973), pp. 4-8.

"Who are the Gifted?" *Instructor*. Vol. 86 (April 1977), p. 55.

Wiener, Gerald. "The Bender Gestalt Test as a Predictor of Minimal Neurologic Deficit in Children Eight to Ten Years of Age." *Nervous and Mental Disease*. Vol. 143 (1966).

Wiig, Elisabeth H. "Language and Learning Disabilities: Identification and Evaluation." *Australian Journal of Remedial Education*. Vol. 8, No. 4 (1976), pp. 4-14.

Wilborn, B.L., and Smith, D.A. "Early identification of children with learning problems; Learning problem indication index." *Academic Therapy*. Vol. 9 (Spring 1974), pp. 363-371.

Williams, J. Floyd. "Learning Disabilities: A Multifaceted Health Threat." *Journal of School Health*. Vol. 46, No. 9 (November 1976), pp. 515-517.

Wilson, John D., et al. "Mission: Audition." *Journal of Special Education*. Vol. 10, No. 1 (Spring 1976), pp. 77-81.

Wilson, J.D., and Spangler, P.F. "Peabody individual achievement test as a clinical tool." *Journal of Learning Disabilities*. Vol. 7 (June 1974), pp. 384-387.

Wissink, J.F., et al. "Bayesian approach to the identification of children with learning disabilities." *Journal of Learning Disabilities*. Vol. 8 (March 1975), pp. 158-166.

Wold, Robert M. "The San Ysidro Study." *Optometric Weekly*. Vol. 62, No. 20 (May 1971), pp. 451-458.

Wolinsky, Gloria F. "Some Factors to Be Considered in Early Pinpointing of a Learning Disabled Child." *Rehabilitation Literature*. Vol. 38, No. 1 (January 1977), pp. 2-4.

Wright, L.S. "Conduct problem or learning disability?" *Journal of Special Education*. Vol. 8 (Winter 1974), pp. 331-336.

Yahraes, Herbert, and Prestwich, Sherry. *Detection and Prevention of Learning Disorders*. National Institute of Mental Health, Rockville, Md., 1976.

Young, Ellery, and Tracy, John M., III. "An Experimental Short Form of the Staggered Spondaic Word List for Learning Disabled Children." *Audiology and Hearing Education*. Vol. 3, No. 1 (December 1977), pp. 7-8, 10-11, 30.

Zahn, Thomas Paul. *Identification of Sensory Motor and Perceptual Limitation. Potential Learning Disability and Hyperkinetic Behavior Disorder in Kindergarten Children*. St. John's University, Jamaica, N.Y., 1975.

Zehrbach, R.R. "Determining a preschool handicapped population; CIP, a comprehensive identification process." *Exceptional Children*. Vol. 42 (October 1975), pp. 76-83.

Zeitlin, Shirley. "Uses and Abuses of Early Identification Programs." Paper presented at an American Psychological Association Symposium on Early Identification for Potential High Risk Learners. 1976.